THE OSHKOSH FLY-IN

BY DON & JULIA DOWNIE

MODERN AVIATION SERIES

TAB BOOKS Inc.

BLUE RIDGE SUMMIT, PA. 17214

FIRST EDITION

FIRST PRINTING

Library of Congress Cataloging in Publication Data

Downie, Don.
    The Oshkosh fly-in.

    Includes index.
    1. Airplanes, Home-built.   2. Experimental Aircraft Association.
    I. Downie, Julia.   II. Title.
TL671.2.D64   629.133'340422   81-9122
ISBN 0-8306-2315-9 (pbk).   AACR2

Contents

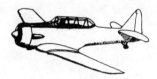

Preface

Commercially-produced airplanes are expensive because they are mostly hand-built. All airplanes are mostly hand-built. There is no other practical way to construct, with the required precision, a framework of maximum strength and minimum weight with the materials available at reasonable cost. Therefore, an individual, working at home, may produce an airplane that in every way rivals the factory-built machines.

Today, the lowest priced light aircraft in the commercial market is nearly $20,000 new. A good two-placer 25 years old will bring $5,000 in the used market. You can build a very nice airplane at home for that amount, and have a machine better suited to your own needs and desires. You may proceed at your own pace and pay as you go. A three-year incubation period is not unusual; neither is the six-month project. Usually, it depends upon the amount of spare time you have, the amount of funds you want to set aside each month for materials, and your level of enthusiasm for the job — assuming that you have chosen a design that is within your perhaps limited range of skills. This latter consideration, along with family (wife or husband) support, are probably the two most important things.

Lack of a "proper" place to work doesn't seem to be much of an obstacle; many a homebuilt airplane has been — and are being — constructed in a living room or bedroom. Most are built in the family garage.

Most amateur plane builders are motivated by factors other than cost alone. Obviously, if you count your labor at $8 per hour (presently, the average starting rate on Cessna's 152 production line), you are not going to save a great deal. However, most figure their labor as part of the fun. In fact, it seems to the authors that one must enjoy working with his hands or a homebuilt airplane project hasn't much chance of being completed. But for those who do, there is a special reward: the feeling that comes from the fact that those sturdy wings out there, taking you so effortlessly over the lush green earth below, are *your own creation*. Just to know that you have created this marvelous machine produces a unique satisfaction that can be fully appreciated only by those who experience it.

There are other practical considerations. With av-gas close to $2 per gallon as this is written, and certain to go much higher, a small, fuel-efficient airplane is the most realistic solution for those who fly for pleasure and on a limited budget.

Also, in recent years, the homebuilt aircraft movement has grown to such proportions that some very talented professional designers have been attracted to it, and as a result it is possible today to construct an airplane at home that is inherently safer, more fuel-efficient, and which returns more performance per horsepower than anything offered in the commercial market. The amateur plane builders are well ahead of the lightplane industry.

Much of the credit for the responsible manner in which the amateur airplane builders in America have and are performing is due to a man by the name of Paul Poberezny, a man with unusual leadership ability and a prodigious amount of common sense. His name will turn up several times in the following pages, because it is not possible to tell the story of Oshkosh, the Experimental Aircraft Association (EAA), and the homebuilt airplane movement without including sport aviation's Maximum Leader.

We should mention that the EAA Headquarters is, at this writing, still at Hales Corners, Wisconsin (P.O. Box 229, Zip 53130), where it has been for more than twenty years. The new facilities at Oshkosh, adjacent to Wittman Field, are expected to be complete late in 1982.

While the EAA started out as a sort of mutual aid society for amateur plane builders, it soon attracted people interested in other forms of sport flying. Restored antique and classic aircraft turned up at the early EAA fly-ins in ever-increasing numbers— everything from civil biplanes built in the mid-twenties to WWII fighters, and that eventually led to the formation of separate divisions within the EAA, the Antique/Classic Division and the EAA Warbirds of America. The amateur aerobatic pilots, or-the International Aerobatic Club, became an EAA division in the early seventies.

Today, the EAA is the spokesman and champion for all forms of sport aviation, and as its membership approaches the 70,000 mark (late 1980), it is well structured, brilliantly directed, and an organization that has become a very significant force in aviation.

Don & Julia Downie

How It All Started

The first airplanes were amateur-built, and many of the basic concepts—from ailerons to tricycle gears to canards, jet propulsion, cantilever wings and monocoque construction—had appeared by 1910, born in the minds of individual constructors. History is *markedly* lacking in examples of human progress through committees.

EARLY HOMEBUILTS

From the end of WWI, the backyard airplane builders were as active as the supply of suitable powerplants would allow. That was a problem that started with the first successful flying machine (the Wrights solved it, sort of, by building their own engine); and development of aircraft propulsion systems have paced the industry ever since. Airplanes are sometimes worse, but never any *better* than the engines that power them.

In 1919, the founders of the WACO company got together in Loraine, Ohio to build a tiny parasol monoplane fitted with a two-cylinder, opposed air-cooled engine (Fig. 1-1). Sam Junkin and Clayton Bruckner would eventually be successful, but their monoplane, and two single-place biplanes that followed, were failures due to lack of a suitable engine.

Clyde Cessna and Matty Laird were among the other pioneers who started with homebuilts and struggled into the air with whatever they could scrounge for power (Fig. 1-2). Laird had a four-cylinder Anzani radial (actually, a pair of two-cylinder V-types, one behind the other, in a single crankcase) which

Fig. 1-1. The first "WACO" was a homebuilt completed in 1919 and fitted with a 30-hp Lawrance two-cylinder opposed engine (courtesy Charles W. Meyers).

vibrated excessively; Cessna used a converted marine engine that imposed a severe weight penalty. Other builders of the period turned to motorcycle engines, the V-types of which could shake the fillings from your teeth, while the four-cylinder Hendersons posed heating problems (Fig. 1-3).

Some of the little homebuilts of the twenties did have potential. The Meyers Midget of 1925 had a speed of 100 mph with a two-cylinder opposed Lawrance engine of 30-hp, although Meyers lost the little biplane to a crash in a railroad yard when the Lawrance failed him (Fig. 1-4). He thereupon built a full-size three-place biplane, powered with a more reliable OX-5 (WW-I surplus) engine—*"reliable"* being a relative description of an airplane engine in those days.

EARLY PRODUCTION LIGHTPLANES

By 1928 some fairly good small radials—LeBlond, Kinner, Warner, Szekely—were being offered in the 40 to 100-hp range, but the price of even the cheapest was beyond the reach of the average amateur plane builder.

Also, by 1928—largely as a result of the tremendous interest in aviation created by Charles Lindbergh's flight to Paris the year before—several small, personal and sport planes appeared: The Driggs Dart, a two-place bipe with a 35-hp Anzani engine, the Elias

Fig. 1-2. E. M. "Matty" Laird began his career as an exhibition pilot in a plane he designed and built himself in 1914. He is seen here (R) with Buck Weaver (at prop, who later founded WACO) at Mission Valley, Iowa County Fair, September, 1915. At left is Ralph McMillan with his Curtiss pusher (courtesy E. M. Laird).

Fig. 1-3. The 1925 Harvey Mummert Sport flew with a V-type motorcycle engine.

Aircoupe, fitted with an 80-hp Anzani, the 30-hp Irwin CC-1, the Mohawk Pinto, low-wing cantilever with an 80-hp Anzani, and the Monocoupe 113, powered with a 60-hp Velie five-cylinder radial. The best and most successful of these was the two-place Monocoupe, designed by Clayton Fokerts and Don Luscombe, priced at $2,675, but in the days of five-cent hamburgers and 25-cent haircuts, that was still too much for most people. Many Monocoupes were sold, with engines eventually ranging up to 125-hp, but they went to the kind of buyer who purchases a new Skyhawk today. (There is an outstanding example of a Monocoupe 113 in the EAA Museum, donated by John Hatz of Merrill, Wisconsin.)

The "standard" open-cockpit biplanes—essentially, Jenny replacements—continued in production from the mid-twenties into the thirties. The WACOs, powered with 90-hp OX-5s and Wright Whirlwinds, the Travel Airs, and Eaglerocks, similarly powered, dominating that market. The two-place Great Lakes came along in 1929 (penalized by its unreliable 90-hp four-cylinder in-line air-cooled Cirrus engine), and the Szekely-powered Curtiss-Wright Junior and Buhl Bull Pup, along with the Aeronca C-3 minimum-horsepower craft, followed in the early thirties. Still, even though the pleasant little C-3 could be bought for $1,790

($450 down, the balance in 12 payments), and the Great Lakes was priced at $3,155 in 1931, the Great Depression left relatively few buyers and the homebuilts began to appeal to more people than ever.

The Pietenpol and Heath

Bernard Pietenpol and Ed Heath came to the rescue of aviation's "little guys" with the Pietenpol Air Camper and the Heath Parasol (Figs. 1-5, 1-6). These were true "Depression airplanes," affordable by just about anyone who really wanted to fly.

The kit for the Heath was offered for $200 less engine, the engine being a four-cylinder air-cooled, in-line motorcycle mill— and the Heath's principal weakness. The Pietenpol, however, was a real down-home, common sense type airplane, with simple all-wood construction and powered by the plentiful and inexpensive Ford Model A engine (Figs. 1-7 through 1-12). True, the Ford carburetor ($1.69 exchange at Sears) tended to cut-out if one nosed-up too sharply, and the Pientenpol's overall performance was right back in the Jenny class—which is to say a cruising speed of 60 mph—but it was an honest, if homely, craft and it put a lot of amateur plane builders into the air. Its Ford engine produced about 35-hp at 1,600 rpm, and although it was heavy, it could be bought new for about $100, and it carried the two-place Pientenpol very well. Bernard Pientenpol recommended 200 hours between overhauls, a job that was normally done in eight hours on this basic hunk

Fig. 1-4. The Meyers Midget of 1926 was fitted with a British-built Cherub engine of 32-hp. Charlie Meyers later designed the WACO Taperwing and, with Cliff Liesey, the Great Lakes 2T-1.

Fig. 1-5. This pair of Pietenpol Air Campers was photographed in the mid-1960s. At left is Allen Rudolph's Model A Ford-powered craft, and (R) a modernized version fitted with a 65-hp Continental owned by Bill Roberts.

of iron. Pietenpol also designed a single-place version of the Air Camper called the Sky Scout which was fitted with a Model T Ford engine, but it was never as popular as the Air Camper.

There would have been a lot more Pietenpols and Heaths and other Depression era homebuilts had it not been for the Federal

Fig. 1-6. Ed Heath's Baby Bullet of 1928 was tailored to Heath's small stature; achieved 140 mph with a 32-hp Bristol Cherub engine.

Fig. 1-7. A Continental-powered Pietenpol flown by Verdell Hallingstad at a Rockford, Illinois fly-in during the early sixties (courtesy Randy Barnes).

Government. The amateur plane builders were wiped out by federal law.

NEW FEDERAL LAWS

What happened was that the 1925 Kelly Bill took the nation's air mail routes away from the Post Office Department (which had pioneered that service during the preceding seven years, mostly with WWI DH-4s), and turned them over to private contractors,

Fig. 1-8. Pietenpol Sky Scout was a single-place version of the Air Camper and powered with a Ford Model T engine.

Fig. 1-9. Sky Scout construction details (courtesy B. H. Pietenpol).

because the Railway Clerks' Union had complained about having to compete with a government department. The private air mail contractors all had visions of empires—*airline* empires—and the mail pay guarantees made it possible, for the first time, to show a profit carrying passengers on a scheduled basis. (The Douglas DC-3, which appeared in 1935, was actually the first transport

Fig. 1-10. Engine installation in the Pietenpol Sky Scout.

Fig. 1-11. During the late sixties, Bernard Pietenpol was flying an Air Camper fitted with a Chevrolet Corvair engine (courtesy B. H. Pietenpol).

airplane that could be operated at a profit with passenger revenues alone.)

However, the investment bankers wanted some law and order brought to the airways before they were willing to put up large sums for the Tri-Motor Fords and Fokkers, and that resulted in the Air Commerce Act of 1926.

It is true that *some* sensible air regulations were needed if civil aviation was to responsibly grow in the United States. It was time

Fig. 1-12. Another Ford A-engined homebuilt was this one-of-a-kind 1933 Manley (courtesy Joe Juptner).

to license pilots, establish testing procedures for the certification of aircraft, and formulate air traffic rules. But the Air Commerce Act contained no provision for the certification of homebuilt airplanes, and without certification they could not legally cross state lines.

THE OREGON HOLDOUTS

That did not immediately ground all homebuilts. The Department of Commerce, charged with enforcing the new law, needed time (and money) to hire inspectors and work out the details of its mandate. However, by 1934 all the states except Oregon had adopted laws that were rubber stamps of the Air Commerce Act and that effectively destroyed the homebuilt movement.

The Oregonians continued to build airplanes in their barns and backyards right up to WWII when *all* private aircraft were grounded in the United States. But the law, and the appearance of the first Piper Cubs, Taylorcrafts and Aeroncas (powered with the new Continental opposed engines of 40-hp, and priced at $1,325 complete), along with an improving economy, left the rest of the country seemingly bereft of private flying's free spirits.

After the war, out of uniform and back at their little airport in Beaverton, Oregon, that group of amateur airplane builders who had held out throughout the thirties, returned to their workshops. Their projects held more potential than ever because, for the first time, proper engines were available at low cost. The 65-hp Continentals and Lycomings, produced in abundance for J-3 Cubs, DE-65 T-crafts and 7AC Aeroncas (L-4s, L-2s and L-3s respectively in Army dress), were ideal for most homebuilt plane projects. Also, a lot of the components from those airplanes were useful to the amateur builder.

The post-war homebuilt movement did not blossom at once. The civil Aeronautics Act of 1938 that created the Civil Aeronautics Administration (CAA), forerunner of the FAA, and took control of civil aviation and the nation's airspace from the Department of Commerce, while generally beneficial to general aviation, still did not recognize that there could be such a thing as a homebuilt airplane. Another factor was the bargains to be had in war surplus training planes. In 1946 one could buy a Vultee BT-13 for as little as $200. However, a boom in agricultural flying soon gobbled up the BT-13s and PR-17s—the BT-13's P&W 450-hp engine installed in the PT-17 airframe making a very good duster/sprayer—and in any case the ex-military planes were too costly to fly and maintain for the average private pilot.

POSTWAR

Meanwhile, several major airframe builders looked at the nearly quarter-million pilots trained by the military during the war and concluded that a post-war boom in private flying was inevitable, and that a new, modern four-placer that could be sold for no more than $10,000 would be just the right merchandise to exploit that market. That decision resulted in the appearance of the Republic SeaBee, Ryan Navion, and Beechcraft Bonanza (all with 165-185 hp engines). But there proved to be no such boom market, and the $9,995 price tags on those aircraft proved unrealistic. The price was too low for the market that actually existed, a market diluted by the Stinson 108 at $4,995, the Super Cub, Ercoupe, and Luscombe at $3,995, and the Piper Cruiser at $3,495.

But a good scrounger could still build an airplane at home for well under $1,000, and there remained a hard core of such people around the country, loosely organized into the American Airmen's Association by George Bogardus of Troutdale, Oregon.

Early in 1946 the members of the American Airmen's Association voted to empty their treasury and send Bogardus to Washington, D.C. in an effort to directly plead the cause of fair play and fun flying to the CAA. Most regarded it as a last resort. But, remarkably, the CAA not only *listened* to Bogardus, but cautiously *agreed* with him. We cannot report the names of those CAA bureaucrats, but the EAA's fine museum should contain their portraits, alongside that of citizen Bogardus.

Anyway, by August, 1947, Bogardus was able to legally fly his homebuilt, the 65-hp "Little Gee Bee," on a transcontinental round-trip with a stop in Washington, where he pushed for specific amendments to the CARs with regard to amateur-built planes. In the beginning, each such aircraft was individually judged by local CAA safety agents, there being no guidelines for the builder to follow. The CAA issued a formal statement, "Safety Regulation Release Number 236," stating that homebuilt aircraft could be certified, although the specifics, as we know them today, had to wait a few more years upon the efforts of citizen Paul Poberezny and his little group in Milwaukee, Wisconsin.

PRESIDENT PAUL

Whatever else may be said about Paul Poberezny (and much is!), certain things cannot be denied. First of all, he is the man who led the sport aviation pilots out of the aeronautical wilderness. He is the one who brought the amateur plane builders' commandments down from the bureaucratic mountain and has jealously guarded them ever since. He is also a man who wouldn't mind in the least being compared to Moses. But if he possesses an ego to match his many abilities, it is artfully disguised—most of the time—by a trait often described as the "common touch." He knows how to communicate with his disciples (Fig. 1-13).

We have observed Paul—and have been fascinated by him—for many years. But there are so many sides to this remarkable man—showman, pilot, administrator, to name just a few tasks at which he excels—and his character seems so complex, that one has difficulty in offering a simple and objective description of him. There is no question but that he tends to be autocratic and runs the EAA with a firm hand. However, that is undoubtedly the only way such a diverse clan may be so successfully handled. Aviation people, generally, are individualists, and none more so than those who build their own airplanes. If you've been around such people for as many years as the authors, you will agree that bringing them together and expecting them to agree on much of *anything* is a Herculean chore in itself. Then, witness how Paul has deftly guided these free spirits, and what he has built with their support, and you *must* respect the guy, whether or not you endorse all his moves.

GROWTH OF THE EAA

The EAA grew from a local group after Paul and a half dozen others in the Milwaukee area got together in 1951 to aid one another with their homebuilt airplane projects. At that time, Paul was on full-time duty flying with the Wisconsin Air National Guard (he has flown everything from jet fighters to four-engine transports). Then, in January, 1953 this group held a formal meeting to organize the Experimental Aircraft Association ("Experimental" because homebuilts are certified in this category by the FAA), and invited others to join. Twenty-five signed up on that snowy evening.

Wisely, the original EAAers did not limit membership to amateur plane builders alone, but welcomes everyone interested in sport flying. Only seven months after that organizational meeting there were 42 members when the first annual fly-in was held; by the end of the year there were 250 EAAers. Paul credits a Leo Kohn story about the EAA, published in the magazine *Mechanix Illustrated*, with bringing in many new members during those early days. Some of the aircraft built by members in the 50s and 60s are shown in Figs. 1-14 through 1-31.

Fig. 1-13. President Paul's Personal P-51. The Mustang features tall Cavalier fin, second seat, and paint scheme of 361st Fighter Group but carries Poberezny's initials instead of correct E2 squadron codes.

A monthly newsletter, the *Experimenter*, grew into a magazine during the fifties and became *Sport Aviation*, which is sent to all paid-up members. This publication has always contained aircraft construction tips, engine data, and stories about interesting homebuilt projects around the country. A series of builder's manuals were also offered.

Another important boost to the growing organization was Paul's personal visits to other cities where he helped in the establishment of local EAA chapters, an activity often facilitated by cross-country flights in the performance of his duties with the Air Guard. Sometimes, he could not stop when or where desired, but on at least one such occasion he let the troops below know that he was thinking of them. We once received a note in the mail from Paul. "It's two a.m., and I'm passing over your town at the controls of a C-47," it read, and he went on to mention the upcoming annual fly-in at Rockford, Illinois, and to congratulate our chapter on its several ongoing homebuilt projects. It was a nice gesture, and an indication of how he paid attention to detail in building the EAA. That happened around 1960, and there were 6,000 members then.

Today, of course, most of Paul's time is taken at Headquarters—and with visits to the FAA in Washington, D.C., where

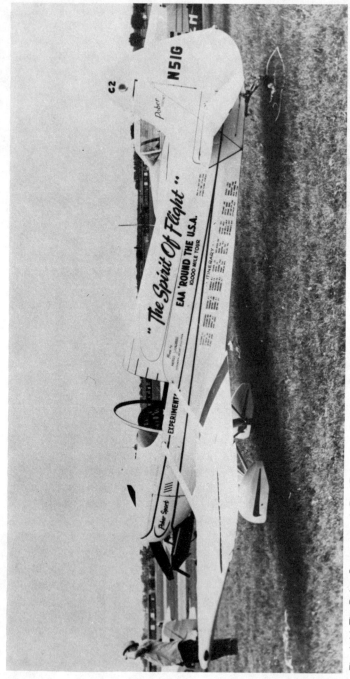

Fig. 1-14. The Pober Sport, an early Paul Poberezny design, toured the USA on an EAA goodwill flight during the fifties (courtesy EAA).

Fig. 1-15. The Meyers Little Toot was a popular homebuilt during the sixties; most were built with 90-hp Continentals. Builder/pilot of this one is Arlo Schroeder of Newton, Kansas (courtesy EAA).

where he keeps EAA fences mended and an eye on any proposed rule changes that might adversely affect sport flying in general and the EAA in particular—and much of the personal contact with members is no longer possible. Late in 1980 there were 66,553

Fig. 1-16. The Corben Baby Ace, a 1930s design, remained popular into the sixties.

Fig. 1-17. Geodetic fuselage construction of this 1950s Sorrell homebuilt provided good strength-to-weight ratio (courtesy Peter M. Bowers).

Fig. 1-18. A one-of-a-kind homebuilt of the early sixties; 65-hp Continental.

Fig. 1-19. Prop-behind-the-tail pushers were rare during the sixties when the Nomad SN-1 appeared at Rockford (courtesy EAA).

paid-up members, and that precluded his personal handling of matters that could be responsibly delegated to others.

Mention of those "others" at EAA Headquarters, or the "Head Shed," could take a book in itself, because Paul has always had interesting and competent people around him. Throughout the fifties, the organization was run by unpaid volunteers. Mrs. Poberezny (Audrey), whom Paul married in 1944 while still in the Air Force, was the business manager. Lois Nolinske, wife of EAA secretary Bob Nolinski, was a sort of Jill-of-all-trades around

Fig. 1-20. Leonard Eaves of Oklahoma City built this folding-wing version of the Nesmith Cougar in the early sixties (courtesy Joe Christy).

Fig. 1-21. The Pitts Special has been popular for 20 years. This one, built by corporate pilot Dean Case of Wichita, Kansas for daughter Joyce was photographed at Tulsa, Oklahoma in 1961 (courtesy Joe Christy).

Fig. 1-22. The Bowers Fly Baby was designed for easy construction, gentle flying characteristics, and with foldable wings for at-home hangaring. All-wood and fabric, it has been popular since its appearance in 1962 (courtesy Peter M. Bowers).

Fig. 1-23. The Knight Twister was the first high-performance homebuilt bipe. Dating from 1934, it was built with many different engines; would do 160 mph with a 90-hp Continental (courtesy Joe Christy).

Headquarters in those days, and Headquarters was in the Poberezny and Nolinski basements. George Hardie, Jr., Val Brugger and S.H. Schmid were responsible for the monthly magazine, which was produced by Ray Scholler of Random Lake,

Fig. 1-24. Paul Poberezny's Baby Ace built in 1959; engine was a 65-hp Continental.

Fig. 1-25. Delta-winged homebuilts began appearing in the early sixties. Pictured is Marion Baker's Delta Kitten, a single-placer with an 85-hp Continental (courtesy Joe Christy).

Wisconsin. There were many others contributing their individual talents, such as "Uncle" Bob Whittier, a sometimes irascible but very knowledgable pilot/mechanic who contributed many fine articles on the subject of low-horsepower aircraft engines.

Fig. 1-26. The Turner T-40 was all-wood and fitted with a 65-hp Continental; designed by Eugene Turner of Ft. Worth in 1960 (courtesy Joe Christy).

Fig. 1-27. The Spezio Tuholer, powered with a Lycoming 0-290G (surplus ground generator plant) of 125-hp. The 0-290Gs are no longer available. The Tuholer was completed in 1962 and a number have been built (courtesy Dorothy Spezio).

Then came the revolution. In the early sixties, some of the other founding members tried to break Paul's firm grip on the organization, charging that he was a dictator and deaf to the ideas of others. Paul saw it differently, of course. As he viewed it, he was the only one who planned big, who was trying to build something worthwhile. The others simply could not grow with the organization, they were content with small plans.

Fig. 1-28. One-of-a-kind Flyrod was photographed at Ottumwa, Iowa, Antique Airplane Association Fly-in, 1966 (courtesy Joe Christy).

29

Fig. 1-29. Parsons-Jocelyn PJ-260, which appeared in the late sixties, shows Great Lakes influence. Engine is a 260-hp Continental (courtesy Peter M. Bowers).

But Paul had enough support to remain in command, and to rewrite the articles of incorporation to allow the election of the directors on a staggered basis so that, in the future, he could avoid the need to confront a whole new board at once. There have been

Fig. 1-30. Pietenpol Air Camper built by Ed Lubitz of Cambridge, Ontario, Canada in 1976. Power is an 85-hp Ford Fiesta engine which consumes 2.8 gph.

Fig. 1-31. A Canadian Davis DA-2A built in 1975, powered with a 90-hp Continental.

no serious challenges to his leadership since that time, and none seem likely.

Paul began drawing a very modest salary in the mid-sixties and some other positions at Headquarters became salaried because, as the membership continued to grow, these became full-time jobs. Paul left the Air Guard in 1969, by which time his position as President of EAA demanded his full attention. By 1975, when the membership passed the 44,000 mark and the EAA was grossing over a million dollars per year, his salary was $36,500 per annum. Three members of his family were also on the payroll, including daughter Bonnie and son Tom.

In 1980, dues from some 66,000 members in 600 local chapters exceeded $1,650,000. The Fly-in at Oshkosh brought in another $1,500,000. Additional income came from admission fees to the EAA Museum where 200 (donated) aircraft and related items are on display; sales from the EAA Gift Shop; sales of EAA manuals and other publications—and contributions.

Where does the money go? Well, it appears that we ain't seen nothin' yet. Paul is still "building something worthwhile." The EAA has acquired 500 acres directly adjacent to Wittman Field in Oshkosh. If you know the layout, it's on the west side of the field. As this is written, hangars, museum, Headquarters building, shops, everything is being constructed there—newer, bigger, better, a permanent home for the EAA of the future. It will be complete by fly-in time, 1982. If you are an EAA member, you'll own a piece of that beautiful new complex.

But don't go trying to tell Paul how to build it; you know how he is.

2

The Membership

Why do people—more than 66,000 of them as this is written—join the EAA? What does the average member get for his/her $25 annual dues? Is Paul Poberezny selling a pipe dream? After all, there clearly are not 66,000 homebuilts flying. The figure is more like 7000.

Well, there is no doubt that in the case of many members a homebuilt airplane parked in the family garage is a dream not likely to be fulfilled. Some join EAA in a short-lived burst of enthusiasm that reality does not sustain. Presumably, many of those drop out. During the almost 30-year history of the EAA approximately 125,000 people have joined. But the normal attrition due to age alone would account for the disappearance of many of those, because the average age of the membership is 38 (about the same as for licensed private pilots in general), so it would seem that EAAers are remarkably constant.

We picked up an EAA "Fact Sheet" at Oshkosh which had this to say under the heading, *EAA Membership Offers Scores of Benefits:* The EAA offers its members a series of excellent publications including *Sport Aviation* magazine. Affiliation with EAA means being part of a successful world-wide team that's tightly bonded by its mutual interest in sport flying. A Washington office is maintained by EAA to insure that its members are represented in the councils of government. EAA membership includes special privileges at fly-ins sponsored by the organization and an opportunity to participate in the educational, developmental and research-oriented activities of the EAA Air Museum Foundation. But more importantly, EAA membership is a passport into the realm of dreamers and doers who share similar interests.

That assessment is much too brief. If you are seriously thinking about building your own airplane, are into antique or classic aircraft; ultralights or Warbirds, you'll find that all have their special programs within the EAA.

THE CHAPTERS

For the first-time plane builder, EAA membership can be very important, especially if one lives in an area where there is a local EAA chapter. Some chapters are large, some small; but all possess experienced people skilled in at least some aspects of aircraft construction. Usually, local chapter members have planes under construction and/or completed and flying. Their help and advice can save the inexperienced plane builder a lot of time, money and unnecessary problems.

Many chapters graft on other activities, particularly for wives, and the regular chapter meetings develop the camaraderie that comes so easily from the gathering of those who share the same interests (Fig. 2-1). Usually, meetings are rotated among members' homes. Some have access to the ground school classrooms of a local FBO. Instructional films are often obtained on a loan basis from the FAA and light aircraft manufacturers, although for the most part such meetings concentrate on demonstrations or discussions of homebuilt aircraft construction materials and techniques by various members of the group.

OBSTACLES

Local chapter support of a member's project can make a lot of difference, not only in the quality of the work, but in seeing the project through to completion. It is estimated that no more than half of all homebuilt airplane projects are ever completed. Too many such dreams never go beyond the planning stage. Still others die slowly during the construction period. Working in one's spare time, and on a pay-as-you-go basis, most projects stretch out into a two to four-year effort, and that requires a certain amount of dedication and sustained enthusiasm that sometimes drops off to zero—especially if one's spouse has been against the idea from the start.

There are no statistics on this latter obstacle, of course, but many veteran EAAers believe that wifely opposition has killed

Fig. 2-1. Many EAA chapters graft-on other activities, particularly those involving wives. This is a corn-on-the-cob feast.

more homebuilt airplane projects than any other single factor. It did appear to us that most homebuilts that turned up at Oshkosh were accompanied by a supportive if not enthusiastic wife—and that would seem to argue heavily in favor of machines of at least two places (and may explain why so many of the successful single-placers are followed by a re-design containing two seats). If a guy has just *got* to have a single-seater, perhaps the way to go is to build *two* of them. There were at least two such husband/wife teams at Oshkosh with "his" and "her" matching airplanes.

Speaking of husband/wife teams, Warren Spencer has a restored Stearman biplane (PT-17) fitted with a 300-hp Lycoming, and wife Ruth has a scaled-down copy of the Stearman which she built herself. It is powered with a 65-hp Continental engine. The Spencers live in Anderson, California and Ruth, a licensed aircraft woodworker, has recently updated and revised her excellent text *Aircraft Dope and Fabric*, TAB book No. 2313.

In addition to the chapter help that many EAA members receive (and give), attendance at the annual fly-in/convention carries special privileges, and the many forums and seminars there, where one may learn construction techniques with various materials and a host of other things related to amateur airplane building, are other benefits to be counted. Also, EAA membership allows admittance to the Oshkosh display areas, and that alone appears to be the reason why many pay their dues. Oshkosh is, after all, the biggest, most complete airshow on earth. It is the annual Pilgrimage To Mecca For The True Believers.

EAA DIVISIONS

Members are attracted to the EAA for other reasons. There are special divisions within the organization for those interested in other forms of sport flying: The Antique/Classic Division, the International Aerobatic Club, the EAA Warbirds of America, and the research programs of the EAA Air Museum Foundation.

Antique/Classic Division

Membership in the Antique/Classic Division costs an extra $14 per year and includes a subscription to *Vintage Airplane* magazine. This division was proposed by Paul in 1971 after he had noticed that more and more antiques and classics were turning up at Oshkosh every year (Figs. 2-2 through 2-9). The EAA had long provided staff help to the antiquers. They were awarded trophies, shown how to conduct forums, provided parking assistance and extended other administrative services. Requests for additional services made it desirable that a separate organization handle their special needs.

Dave Jameson was the first president of the organization, followed by E. E. "Buck" Hilbert who was in turn succeeded by J. R. Nielander, Jr. The current president is W. Brad Thomas, Jr. While the leadership has changed hands over the years, the objectives of the Antique/Classic Division remain as established on 6 November 1971, the day the division was founded:

1. Encourage and aid in the retention and restoration of antique and classic aircraft.

2. Establish a library devoted to the history of aviation and to the construction, repair, restoration, maintenance and preservation of antique and classic aircraft and engines.

3. Hold the conduct meetings, displays and educational programs relating to aviation with emphasis on restoration, maintenance, and care of antique and classic aircraft and engines.

4. Improve aviation safety and aviation education with reference to antique and classic aircraft.

Generally, *antique* aircraft include those constructed by the original manufacturer on or before 31 December 1945. Aircraft

Fig. 2-2. Aeronca Chief (L) and Aeronca Sedan; two beautiful examples of restored classics.

constructed by the original manufacturer between 1 January 1946 and 31 December 1955 are classified as *classics*.

Membership in the Antique/Classic Division is open to anyone interested in vintage aircraft. Some of the members believe in restoring the old machines and saving them for posterity; others

Fig. 2-3. The Ford Trimotor is an antique. Approximately 200 were built between 1926 and 1932 inclusive. Passenger capacity is 12 to 16. This one was restored at a cost of $300,000; sold new for $50,000.

Fig. 2-4. The Temco Swift CG-1B has 125-hp, is two-place, cruises at 140 mph, and was built by the Texas Engineering Manufacturing Company of Dallas between 1946 and 1950 inclusive. Sign on the tethered balloon is "Join EAA." From a distance it was mis-read by a few.

Fig. 2-5. Wilbur Draves' 65-hp Mooney Mite. These little plywood-covered single-placers cruise at 125 and were produced 1950 to 1955 inclusive.

Fig. 2-6. Paul Ristin, a WW-II B-17 pilot, and his 1946 Culver V, an airplane designed by Al Mooney.

Fig. 2-7. This 1911 Curtiss pusher is powered with a Curtiss OX engine of 1916 vintage.

Fig. 2-8. Aeronca C-2, part of the EAA Museum permanent display, belongs to E. E. "Bud" Herbert of Union, Iowa. The C-2, with 26-hp Aeronca engine, sold for $1,245 new in 1931.

want to keep them flying. But the majority seem to just want to share a part of aviation heritage with like-minded people. Whether they restore, maintain, fly or simply admire (perhaps with a touch of nostalgia) the old birds, these members are often the most

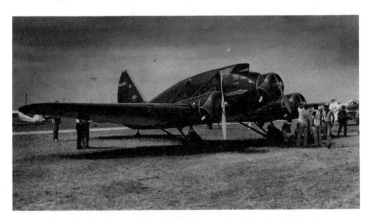

Fig. 2-9. Stinson Model A eight-passenger airliner refurbished as it looked when in service with American Airlines in 1935. Original engines were 260-hp Lycomings which provided a cruise of 160 mph.

devoted of all EAAers and derive a lot of pleasure from getting together.

The Antique/Classic Division plays a major role nowadays in the annual fly-in/convention at Oshkosh. Members supervise and operate the antique and classic display areas. They also organize and schedule scores of forums and seminars on various phases of maintenance and restoration on a variety of antique and classic aircraft. Additionally, the division recognizes the best of the restorer's art by awarding EAA trophies in many categories and classifications. In this way, excellence and authenticity in restoration is encouraged. Many members have been instrumental in obtaining books, manuals and other aviation memorabilia for the EAA Air Museum Library, an excellent reference source.

A minimum of five members may establish an EAA Antique/Classic local chapter. The A/C Division Headquarters staff handles correspondence, maintains membership lists, purchases supplies and merchandise, provides computer and accounting services and handles promotion.

International Aerobatic Club

The International Aerobatic Club is a division of the EAA and was incorporated in 1970. (There is also an Aerobatic Club of America which preceded formation of the IAC and which has no connection with the EAA.) The EAA had a legitimate interest in aerobatics because most of the aerobatic airplanes in the U.S. were homebuilts, and Paul Poberezny, worried that the amateur acro pilots could jeopardize the safety record of the EAA in general, decided that the tumble-types should be encouraged to follow the safety practices of the professionals and that, given their own organization, they could establish high standards and follow a system of self-policing that would benefit all concerned.

Membership in the EAA's IAC costs $24 per year, including EAA membership and the monthly publication *Sport Aerobatics*. An additional $14 includes *Sport Aviation* magazine. Anyone with a sincere interest in sport aerobatics may join.

The charter members were experienced acro pilots, and they shared a compelling desire to establish aerobatics as a safe art, a sane sport, and a sure method of increasing pilot proficiency.

IAC President Carl Bury lists this division's goals as:

1. Promote grass roots aerobatics.

2. Provide educational and instructional material.

3. Provide technical information, advice and suggestions.

4. Provide safety for both pilots and aircraft.

5. Encourage an aerobatic judges' school.

6. Establish definite, clear-cut rules for competition.

7. Sponsor a multitude of contests, enabling as many pilots as possible to participate.

8. Bring the fun, fellowship and thrill of aerobatics and sport flying to as many people as possible.

Four proficiency levels have been established by the IAC for the more than 30 local and regional aerobatic contests held each year, Sportsman, Intermediate, Advanced, and Unlimited. At each contest IAC members are given an opportunity to measure flying skills against an established system of grading and earn aerobatic achievement awards. Certificates, plaques and trophies may be earned. Judging and ground-assist operations offer the non-competing members a chance to participate.

Membership in the IAC includes eligibility in all IAC sanctioned events. Upon request, official contest rules are available, and as a division of the EAA, the International Aerobatic Club draws upon the parent organization's staff and services to handle its correspondence, maintain membership lists, provide computer and accounting services and handle promotions.

Warbirds of America

Membership in the EAA Warbirds of America Division costs an extra $20 per year over and above one's annual $25 EAA dues, and includes a subscription to the monthly *Warbird Newsletter.*

Warbirds of America began as an independent organization in the early sixties, dedicated to flight safety and improvement of piloting skills. Membership was limited to those who possessed WWII aircraft of more than 600 hp. In 1970 they were incorporated as an EAA division and their ranks opened to all who have an interest in WWII era military aircraft. Once under the administrative wing of the EAA, the Warbirds flourished and brought to the EAA their determination to preserve the old military aircraft.

Fellowship and mutual support is the bond that brings the Warbirds together, as with all EAA divisions, and it springs from a fascination and respect for one of the most thrilling chapters in the history of manned flight. A few members may see dollar signs dancing before their eyes, because a well-restored World War Two airplane may be worth a king's ransom, but that was *not* the reason the Warbirds organized in the first place, nor is it the primary motivating factor among them today.

Although the emphasis has always been on finding, obtaining, restoring, preserving and flying WW-II era combat aircraft and trainers, the members share other interests. In recent years military airplanes of later vintage such as the T-28, A-1 Skyraider, and T-34 have taken their places next to the Bell Airacobras, North American Mustangs, Grumman Hellcats and Wildcats, Supermarine Spitfires, Lockheed Lightnings and Curtiss Warhawks (Figs. 2-10 through 2-13).

While some Warbird members own their own aircraft, most help in the maintenance or restoration of someone else's bird. Many others join Warbirds merely to support and to be associated with an organization that encourages the preservation of part of aviation's military heritage. In other words, the organization is open to all men and women who own, fly or are interested in military aircraft.

Warbirds is an international organization, with members in all 50 states, Canada, Mexico, and several overseas countries. Since they are so widely scattered, they concentrate on individual participation in air shows rather than a fully orchestrated performance in a single location. Officially, they list their goals as:

1. Promote and encourage the preservation and operation of WWII era aircraft.

2. Educate members and non-members in methods of safe operation and maintenance of wartime aircraft.

3. Organize and promote static displays and other public demonstrations.

4. Establish, operate and maintain a flight and static museum, dedicated to WWII aircraft, as part of the EAA Air Museum Foundation.

EAA Air Museum Foundation

The EAA's museum, officially the Paul H. Poberezny Air Museum, is located at 11311 West Forest Home Avenue in Franklin, Wisconsin, a southwest Milwaukee suburb, but will be in new and expanded quarters adjacent to Wittman Field, Oshkosh, Wisconsin by the end of 1982. It is the centerpiece of the EAA Air Museum Foundation, which was established in 1962 to foster research and educational programs in aviation at the grass roots level. The Foundation is funded through contributions, profits derived from the Air Museum Gift Shop, and the sale of EAA technical publications.

The Foundation's museum houses the world's largest private collection of aircraft and artifacts, and is unique among air

Fig. 2-10. A Lockheed P-38 Lightning is a rare sight today. If the Air Force serial number on its tail is correct, this example is a P-38L-5. The L model Lightnings entered service in the Southwest Pacific with the 5th Air Force in mid-October 1944.

museums for its focus on amateur-built aircraft. The collection includes nearly 200 aircraft and related articles, among which are exact replicas of the Wright brothers' Flyer and Lindbergh's Spirit of St. Louis. There are antique aircraft, racers, warbirds, early

Fig. 2-11. A pair of Hawker Sea Furies leads parade of WW-II fighters as they taxi out for a fly-by. The Sea Fury was a redesign of the earlier Hawker Tempest and had a top speed of 438 mph at 21,000 ft. It appeared too late for combat in WW-II, but saw service in the Korean War with the British Navy.

Fig. 2-12. North American T-28s, post-war trainers.

homebuilts, aerobatic aircraft and early commercial biplanes. Model buffs should appreciate the scale model display depicting the development of airline transportation.

A little known function of the museum is its shops where significant aircraft are restored. Other activities include the sponsorship of seminars and workshops.

Project Schoolflight is the foundation's outreach program. As the name implies, it focuses on students and was started in 1973 "to encourage pride in craftsmanship in the younger generation." Since then, more than 350 high schools, vocational schools, and colleges have undertaken aircraft construction projects. Using

Fig.2-13. The Temco T-35 Buckaroo prototype was built in 1950 as a military trainer and light attack aircraft, but never produced. Engine is a 210-hp IO-360D. The Air Force and Navy bought instead the Beechcraft T-34, a militarized Bonanza.

EAA Foundation specially developed aircraft designs and plans, students learn the basic techniques of woodworking, sheetmetal work, steel tube assembly, as well as electrical, hydraulic and finishing operations. These basic and essential skills spill over to

Fig. 2-14. The Mother Earth News comes to Oshkosh to demonstrate how one may distill his own alcohol fuel—the only alcoholic brew allowed at the EAA Fly-in Convention.

Fig. 2-15. A homebuilt airplane under construction as a "Project Schoolflight" activity sponsored by the EAA Museum Foundation.

Fig. 2-16. The interest in fabric-covered aircraft is evidenced by the popularity of the wing covering workshop at Oshkosh.

Fig. 2-17. Fabric rib-stitching at one the many workshops at Oshkosh sponsored by the EAA Museum Foundation and manned by EAA volunteers.

Fig. 2-18. The ultralights continue to proliferate at Oshkosh and an Ultralight Division within the EAA was announced in August, 1980.

Fig. 2-19. The Rotec Rally 2B has a three-axis control system and 17-hp. Construction kit sells for $3,280; ready to fly the Rally sells for $3,580.

other avocations, and many Project Schoolflight graduates have gone on to careers in aviation as engineers and mechanics.

Project Schoolflight is always in need of more volunteers to act as Technical Representatives. These people come from the ranks of the EAA. Some are schoolteachers, FAA personnel, FBOs or just plain aviation enthusiasts with skills or knowledge that allows them to promote aviation in their local schools and perhaps advise on the ongoing programs.

Project Schoolflight also applies to youth clubs. Many youth clubs have started building airplanes and many have finished them. The Foundation supports the goals of the Civil Air Patrol, Aviation Explorers, and other youth groups interest in aircraft building.

The Foundation's Flight Research Center is currently working to find alternative energy sources as aircraft fuels. A program to get a Cessna 150 certified to operate on automobile gasoline has been in the works for more than a year. Tests with gasohol, alcohol (Fig. 2-14) and other fuels are encouraged through the Foundation's representation on the General Aviation Energy Council, chaired by Paul Poberezny. A variety of other projects affecting sport aviation are always under review by the research center.

During each fly-in/convention at Oshkosh, the Air Museum sponsors a series of workshops for the benefit of EAA members. Welding for the novice and the experienced is featured with hands-on sessions under expert guidance. The Wood Shop features the building of a complete major component such as a fuselage or wing and demonstrates propeller carving techniques. The Metal Shop (Fig. 2-15) also builds a complete airframe component, while the Synthetics Workshop offers demonstrations in a variety of processes, fiberglass, foam and epoxies in a forum-type program during which a number of components are completed. The Fabric Shop (Fig. 2-16) teaches rib-stitching (Fig. 2-17), taping, gluing, doping and painting, while the engine workshops—there are always several—detail the many ways to modify auto engines for aircraft use.

EAA Ultralight Division

News flash: "Oshkosh, Wisconsin, 6 August 1980 . . . Paul H. Poberezny, president of the Experimental Aircraft Association, announced today that the worldwide sport aviation organization's Board of Directors had approved a new ultralight division . . . (Figs. 2-18, 2-19).

" 'We're extending an invitation to the growing number of ultralight enthusiasts to join the world's largest sport aviation group,' said Poberenzy. 'We feel the incorporation of an ultralight division in EAA will prove mutually beneficial. It will give the ultralight movement a recognized and respected voice in aviation and it will infuse EAA membership rolls with the youthful energy and enthusiasm so characteristic of ultralight pilots.' "

3

Is It For Me?

Perhaps most people who give any thought to the idea of building a personal airplane begin with such basic questions as *could I really do it? How much labor and expense is involved? How long will it take?* And *what's my wife going to say about it?*

Only the first and the last of these questions will have definite answers. To the first, the answer is, *yes, you can really do it*, assuming that you are a reasonably normal human being. As for how your wife will react, well, she's *your* wife; you can answer that better than we can.

How much labor is involved? Probably more than you expect. But as homebuilt airplane designer/builder Peter Bowers once observed, building an airplane is not a big job; it is a collection of little ones—a *lot* of little ones. *That is what makes it managable.*

BUILDING YOUR PERSONAL AIRPLANE

The number of problems one may encounter, which is to say the degree of difficulty faced on any given project, will be determined by several factors. First, it is almost an imperative that you enjoy creating things. If you like to work with your hands, chances are that the other factors will be secondary and the problems will submit to common sense solutions. The satisfaction to be derived from working with one's hands appears to be the one common denominator among amateur aircraft builders—in addition, of course, to their mutual love of the sky and all things that fly. In most other ways they are a diverse bunch. Every profession, every trade, every economic level, male and female, is represented among those flying homebuilt airplanes.

Actually, homebuilt airplane projects today are both better and easier than in past years. The designs are better because some very talented aircraft engineers have been attracted to this market, while both materials and techniques, suited to limited skills and limited equipment, have evolved (Fig. 3-1).

Also, the FAA is much more experienced in this field, and every GADO (General Aviation District Office) will have at least one inspector familiar with homebuilts. The GADO should be your starting point (following, or concurrent with attendance at local EAA chapter meetings). The FAA inspectors there will check your work at least twice during the construction period, and you must have their approval to fly your creation. They are *not* fond of surprises, so let them know what you intend to do from the beginning. Moreover, since they have similarly handled all the other homebuilts in your district, their advice can be very useful. They will know of any problems encountered in the building and flying of those designs. Their advice doesn't cost anything, so see them before you buy a set of plans or the first batch of components for kit construction. Between the FAA inspectors and the reachable amateur plane builders in your vicinity, you should gain a solid foundation of basic data to get you properly started before you clean out the family garage and begin your great adventure.

Fig. 3-1. Wittman Tailwind has been a popular design since the mid-fifties as a result of good performance and relative ease of construction.

SELECTING A DESIGN

Several factors must be considered in design selection. Among them is type of construction, number of seats, and the availability and cost of a proper engine. Acquisition of an acceptable engine is often the biggest problem faced by the amateur plane builder, and it can go a long way toward determining the design you ultimately select.

The ultralights have a number of chainsaw and snowmobile engines for power (Fig. 3-2), but the average single or two-place homebuilt airplane requires more horsepower. In the 50 to 70-hp range, the converted VWs appear to be the most practical, least expensive, and most numerous, especially the Monnett conversion. But engines of 100-hp and above, almost exclusively Continental and Lycoming aircraft engines, are *expensive*. Currently, a freshly-majored 0-200 (100-hp), 0-235 (108-115 hp), 0-290D (125-135 hp), or 0-320 (150-hp) are priced in the $5,000 range. Used ones will range upward from about $2,000, depending upon condition and accessories.

RotorWay has recently entered this market with a 100-hp liquid-cooled engine intended for amateur-built planes (Figs. 3-3, and 3-4). It weighs 170 lbs dry and will burn 100 octane av-gas or automotive fuel of 92 octane or better. It sells for $4,500 without accessories and, at this writing, has not flown long enough in enough homebuilts for us to offer a solid appraisal of its performance.

One small bright spot in the engine picture for the future is the fact that the trusty 0-235 Lycoming, which first appeared in the mid-forties, seems destined to remain in production for some time to come because it is used by both the Beechcraft Skipper and the Piper Tomahawk trainers. Some of these engines, which powered a lot of Citabrias, Yankees and others, will be available in the used market, and are rated on 80/87 octane red av-gas. The late models of the 0-235 are rated for 100 octane low lead (LL100) blue av-gas, which will eventually be the standard fuel for all general aviation piston-engines if the oil companies have their way.

There have already been shortages of 80/87 red and it will almost certainly disappear altogether by the end of this decade. By this time, gen-av pilots have had enough experience operating 80-octane engines on LL100 blue to know that it burns exhaust valves and fouls spark plugs. Although LL100 blue is called "low lead," it is low lead only in comparison to 100/130 green. It contains about half as much tetraethyl lead (TEL) as 100/130 green, but it contains twice as much TEL as 80/87 red. *This* is progress?

We once spent an afternoon with a petroleum chemist in an effort to learn just why, exactly, automobile gasoline should not be used as an aircraft fuel. He said some things we did not understand too well, but finally summed up his reply by saying that the unstable olefin hydrocarbons in automobile gasoline cause gum deposits and are susceptible to vapor lock because of a relatively low boiling point. Av-gas, largely composed of high heat energy paraffins, resists vapor lock with a 140-deg F boiling point at sea level, 100-deg at 20,000 ft, and additives give it other desirable properties such as resistance to plug fouling and support its octane rating at rich mixtures. Vapor lock (gasoline boiling in the fuel lines) is not considered likely at pressure altitudes below 5,000 ft, and perhaps that has been the starting point for the EAA's research with auto gas in a Cessna 150. Some of the VW-powered homebuilts are flown on auto gas, although the Monnett people say they usually burn LL100 in their own airplanes.

CONSTRUCTION CONSIDERATIONS

Amateur-built airplanes have taken shape in some very unlikely places, proving that a formal shop is not absolutely

Fig. 3-2. The powered hang gliders have come a long way from the flex-wing hang gliders that gave birth to this exciting sport.

Fig. 3-3. The 100-hp RotorWay water-cooled engine has been designed and marketed especially for homebuilt aircraft and is rated on either aviation or automobile gasoline.

54

Fig. 3-4. Rotorway RW-100 engine installed in a Rutan design.

necessary. We know of an airline pilot who built an airplane in his bedroom (he's not married). Ruth Spencer built "Broomstick" in her living room and basement. And when we asked Dorothy Spezio about the construction of husband Tony's airplane, she said, "Let me tell you about *our* airplane!

"I was against it at first," she confessed. "After Tony had his plans, he started bringing in the junk, or *'goodies'* as they were known around our house, like a squirrel storing nuts for the winter . . .

"But I finally became accustomed to finding Tony's bureau drawers stuffed with airplane fabric and pinked tape and second-hand airplane instruments."

She went on to say that the wing ribs were made on the kitchen table; tail surfaces were made upstairs, covered in their living room, doped in the garage, and hung in the bathroom to dry. You can see the results in Fig. 3-5.

The smell of aircraft dope in the house is a *real* test of a marriage, it seems to us. Building inside the home has got to be a last resort, and only if there are no children and both husband and wife are equally dedicated to the task.

You should have a space where the work can be left standing, and an area the size of a one-car garage is about minimum. You must have enough space to lay out and construct the wing panels and fuselage on saw horses, with ample room on all sides. It is probably best to build the wings and tail surfaces first since those completed components may be suspended vertically by their aileron hinges and attachment fittings and will take up little space.

You will work more efficiently if the floor is kept clean and the workspace is uncluttered. Have a place for each tool and *always* return each tool to its place. You must be "organized" in order to make the most of your time. Above all, carefully plan each operation *before* you begin it.

Sometimes, visitors are a problem, and that may even include fellow EAAers. Those who have airplane-building experience can be very helpful. Others may simply drink your beer and keep you from working. One builder we know printed a three-foot sign which he tacked to the back wall of his garage:

NOTICE TO FRIENDS, VISITORS, RELATIVES AND OTHER AIRPLANE PEOPLE: WELCOME TO THE JACK CUNNINGHAM AIRPLANE WORKS! I ENJOY YOUR COMPANY AND APPRECIATE YOUR IN-TEREST. BUT IF I STOP TO CHAT OR ANSWER QUESTIONS I'LL NEVER GET THIS THING BUILT! PLEASE UNDERSTAND!

A personal note: Since your wife's support of the project is a critical factor to its ultimate success, *never* force her to change or

Fig. 3-5. The Spezio Tuholer (two open cockpits, hence, two holes) components were partly constructed in the Spezio home.

cancel plans so that you can work on the airplane. Also, continue to perform all your normal chores around the house: keep the lawn mowed, the shrubbery trimmed and sprayed, take out the trash, and so forth. In fact, this can be a good time to inject fresh meaning into your relationship. Tell her how much you appreciate her support and show it with a little surprise gift now and then. After all, the money you are spending on the airplane could have gone for some things *she* may have preferred. Make it clear that she is more important to you than the airplane.

Doping or painting should not be done in a confined area without adequate ventilation; and since glue and other liquids have a working-temperature range between 70 and 90-deg F, you must also have temperature control as well as humidity control or else wait for benign weather conditions.

TOOLS

Some airplanes are built with a bare minimum of tools; some types of construction require relatively few tools, but you will simplify the job and save time if your tools reasonably match the type of construction you have selected. Basic woodworking tools should be on your pegboard whatever the materials to be employed. Some woodworking is necessary even on all-metal airplanes because jigs and pattern blocks are needed.

The pop riveter has made all-metal homebuilts practical, along with designs that require no fancy bending of the components or compound curves of the skin. Wood and fabric construction is well suited to a minimum home workshop, and designs such as the Bowers Fly Baby, actually just an outsized model airplane, have been popular for that reason (Fig. 3-6). Welded steel tube

Fig. 3-6. Construction of the all-wood Bowers Fly Baby has been compared to the building of an oversize model airplane.

fuselages are losing favor because the cost of 4130 chrome moly tubing is approaching the ridiculous, and most amateur builders have to hire the welding done. Shaped styrofoam blocks over a wooden frame, covered with dynel fabric and epoxy resin, is a simple process that is gaining in popularity. Variations of foam, fiberglass cloth and epoxies, over a wooden substructure, are featured in many of today's homebuilt designs (Fig. 3-7). These materials are easy to work, require a minimum of tools and no previous building experience. The resulting airframes are strong, light, and have very smooth surfaces.

The following tools should be considered essential:

- ☐ Hacksaw.
- ☐ Hand saw.
- ☐ Table or radial arm power saw.
- ☐ Electric hand drill and bits to maximum diameter of ⅜-inch.
- ☐ Files: flat, rounded and rat tail.
- ☐ Bench vice.
- ☐ C-clamps.
- ☐ Tin snips.
- ☐ Saw horses, at least two.
- ☐ Standard and Phillips screwdrivers.
- ☐ Pliers.
- ☐ Diagonal cutters ("dikes").
- ☐ Glue and dope brushes; assorted sandpaper.
- ☐ Carpenter's level.
- ☐ Combination square.
- ☐ Steel measuring tape, six foot.
- ☐ Sailmaker's needles (for fabric-covered aircraft).
- ☐ Sheet metal fasteners (for metal skins).
- ☐ Pop riveter (for metal skins).
- ☐ Box or open-end wrenches to ¾-inch.

In addition to the above, a drill press and bench grinder can be very useful.

LEGAL CONSIDERATIONS

Homebuilt aircraft are licensed in the "Experimental" category by the FAA. There are a number of sub-classifications in this category. A standard production airplane with significant modifications (a clipped-wing Cub, for example) may be certified as Experimental. The amateur-built airplane is in the sub-classification titled "For Recreation and Educational Purposes."

When homebuilts were first certified back in the late forties, some people put together airplanes by simply collecting components of production aircraft. A lot of Cub and Aeronca wings turned up on homemade fuselages. But the FAA ruled out that approach long ago. One may use fuel tanks, engine mounts, engines, all kinds of standard aircraft hardware, even landing gear, from production airplanes without violating the spirit or intent of the FARs, but no *major* components such as wings, fuselage, etc., may be employed. You can still put together an airplane that way, but it won't be certified as a homebuilt and will be specifically limited to the use for which it is built such as airshow work. Again, any time you contemplate leaving the beaten track in the building or modification of an airplane, you will be wise to first discuss the planned project with the people in the nearest GADO. It may save you both money and a lot of wasted effort.

In addition to the Experimental category, and the Standard category for production aircraft, the FAA also certifies airplanes in the Limited and Restricted categories for special purposes. But our concern here is homebuilts.

Homebuilts may *not* be flown for hire, rented, leased, or used for commercial purposes, although you are allowed to use them for

Fig. 3-7. The designs of Burt Rutan (pointing) have greatly impacted the homebuilt scene because of their efficiency, safety, and ease of construction with non-traditional materials. Brother Dick Rutan (center) and Mike Melvill ponder Burt's directions.

personal transportation when travelling on business. This is important because it allows you to deduct fuel and oil as a legitimate business expense. Whether or not you may also crank in depreciation on the airplane, insurance and related costs, may be debatable with the IRS, and although common sense has nothing to do with income taxes, such allowances do seem reasonable.

Homebuilts may be flown in airshows only if there is no payment for such appearances.

Normally, homebuilts are restricted to daylight VFR only; but they may be approved for night operation if properly equipped.

Student pilots—that is, a solo student flying on a valid Student's Permit—may fly a homebuilt if he/she has been "signed off" to fly that particular airplane by a qualified flight instructor. This isn't much of a problem with a gentle machine like a Bowers Fly Baby, but probably cannot (and *should* not) be done on high-performance homebuilts.

PAPERWORK

At the risk of sounding like a broken record, we say again, consult the GADO people from the very beginning of your homebuilt airplane project. Another reason for this is the paperwork required to make your airplane legal. As one wag put it, "When the weight of the paperwork equals the weight of the aircraft, you may legally fly it." The way to sail through the paperwork without problems and delays is to be in touch with those who require all those forms.

Designation: To begin with, you will have to identify your homebuilt with a make and model designation, and give it a serial number. If you designed the airplane yourself, you provide the make, model and serial, e.g., the "Downie Wombat D-1, serial #1." If the plane was built from plans or a kit without alteration, these data are supplied by the plans seller. If you have significantly altered the original design, then you add your name to that of the designer ("Downie-Wittman Tailwind") and provide your own model and serial number. It is not a good idea to alter purchased plans without first consulting with your friendly neighborhood GADO. The substitution of materials or even a change in the size of a structural part may not be approved by the FAA inspector, and it is a lot cheaper to find that out *before* you make the change.

A metal plate must be permanently affixed to the airframe, usually on the instrument panel, which is stamped with the make, model, serial number, name and address of the builder, along with the date the airplane was completed. You can obtain blank plates for this purpose from the EAA.

Logbooks: Your machine must have two logbooks (unless it is a sailplane, which needs only one, or a powered hang glider which, at this writing, needs none). One is the *engine* log, the other the *airframe* log. All flight time, mishaps, repairs, modifications, added equipment, and inspections must be logged and available for inspection by the FAA. These are *legal documents required by law*, therefore, it is a misdemeanor to tamper with the facts when making entries in them. These books are obtainable at any airport, although the EAA sells engine and airframe logs especially suited to homebuilts.

Initial FAA Inspection: An FAA inspector must check your airplane before the cover goes on, or at whatever stage of the construction he chooses. He may check the work more than once. Make sure that such inspections are entered in the airframe log and signed by the inspector, because it is entirely possible that a different inspector will show up for the final inspection when you are ready to test-fly the machine. If your design calls for a box spar or other type of enclosed component, *don't close it until the inspector has seen it.*

Registration: You will need several special FAA forms which are obtainable at the nearest FAA office. These include the Aircraft Registration Application, which must be filled out and sent (with $5) to the FAA Aircraft Registry, P. O. Box 25504, Oklahoma City, OK 73125. Accompanying this application will be proof of ownership. When you purchase a plane, new or used, this requirement is satisfied by filling out FAA Form 8050-2 (Bill of Sale), but when you register an airplane you have built yourself you'll need an "affidavit of original construction," a notarized letter attesting to that fact, accompanied by identification drawings or photographs that allow the FAA to establish a record of positive identification. As your project nears completion, you'll write a formal letter requesting designation of a test area, which will go to the nearest FAA Air Traffic Supervisor; and the Airworthiness Certificate Application will follow when your airplane is ready to fly. The Airworthiness Certificate itself will be filled out by the inspector when he gives approval for the first flight after a final inspection.

Finally, after you have flown the 50-75 hours in the test area, you will write another letter confirming that fact and requesting that the test restrictions be lifted.

The following regulations are applicable to an applicant for an experimental certificate:

☐ The appropriate sections of FAR Part 47, Aircraft Registration, which prescribes the requirements for obtaining an identification number and registering the aircraft. Section 47.33 applies specifically to registration of homebuilts.

☐ FAR Part 21, Section 21.182 prescribes identification requirements.

☐ FAR Part 45 establishes requirements for data and location of identification plates, display of Airworthiness Certificates and display of the identification number.

☐ FAR Part 21, Sections 21.173 and 21.193 give the requirements for submittal of an application for the Airworthiness Certificate.

Plans: Unfortunately, not everyone contemplating the construction of a homebuilt aircraft is armed with all the information he/she should have in order to avoid some of the pitfalls. This is the principal reason that one should become associated with an EAA chapter if possible. Those who have been over the road can identify the rough spots. One of those spots is the chance of a rip-off by a plans seller. There appears to be no way to prevent anyone from dreaming-up an attractive-looking airplane and offering plans for it *even though no prototype has been built.* There is no law that requires that plans be complete, or even practical for home construction.

This problem was recognized some time ago and the National Assocation of Sport Aircraft Designers (NASAD), a non-profit, voluntary group, was organized in an attempt to establish some standards that would protect the unwary plans buyers.

NASAD has helped. So has the EAA by being careful about which advertisements for plans it accepts in Sport Aviation. But there are a lot of other aviation publications which do not screen plans advertisers; and NASAD is limited in its effectiveness because its members, who serve without pay, obviously cannot court lawsuits, and evaluate only those plans submitted by the sellers.

THE WARBIRDS

The people who restore and fly WWII airplanes just have to be considered a tad exclusive, and the only thing they have in common with the amateur plane builders is a mutual love for airplanes—albeit a very difficult kind of airplanes.

Back in the later sixties, we visited the Confederate Air Force Headquarters down in the sourthern tip of Texas. The CAF even then possessed the best collection of WWII airplanes in the U.S. We came away convinced that this was a great bunch of colonels (in the CAF everyone is a "colonel"); but we also left them with a nagging suspicion that we had missed something. It was the kind of feeling you get after buying something you didn't intend to buy but find yourself convinced by a very personable salesman. Everything they said about CAF aims was logical and laudable. Then why the unbidden thought that this dedicated bunch just might be laying a classic snow job on the USAF, the IRS, gullible aviation writers, and all those warbird lovers contributing time and money to "keep the historic combat aircraft flying for posterity?"

Our suspicion was probably rooted in the fact that the CAF flew the planes instead of merely preserving them. A handful of CAF colonels was having all the fun while being subsidized by a lot of sincere people who believed in the CAF's stated aims.

The CAF countered by pointing out that a *flying* museum was the whole idea behind their effort; that one has got to hear those Merlins and Double Wasps winding up, and see these planes in flight to truly capture the essence of that era. They are presenting *living* history, they will tell you, in a way that photographs, motion pictures or static displays cannot match.

They point out that the airplanes owned by the CAF Museum are far too valuable to be flown by any but the colonels who are well qualified and who have invested their own labor in the restorations; and some machines are owned by individuals who have borne their own restoration costs. Therefore, a lot of CAF colonels never log time in a P-38 or even get to ride in the CAF B-17s. The main benefit to most contributors is the satisfaction they derive from knowing that they are helping to preserve the CAF's aircraft in flying condition.

That is enough for a lot of people because, on an individual basis, there is more to the Warbird movement than meets the eye. These old warplanes hold a deep attraction for many people (including your authors and editors). It can't be simple nostalgia because so many who own and fly them were not even born until after WWII, nor is it, in most cases, the expectation of a big profit. True, a well restored Warbird may bring an unbelievable price—currently, as much as $200,000 for, say, a P-47 Thunderbolt—but the cost of restoration is usually equally unbelievable; and it appears to us that relatively few Warbird owners are anxious to sell.

On a flight from Florida to California recently, we stopped in Lawton, Oklahoma to spend an evening with TAB's aviation editor, Joe Christy, and his wife Rene, and at Lawton Municipal admired the newly-restored B-25J Mitchell owned by the Cunningham brothers who operate an agricultural aviation service there. Ray Cunningham was working on one of his ag-planes, but stopped to talk with us when he noticed our interest in his B-25. He had located it via the av-grapevine early in 1979, after restoring an L-2 Taylorcraft liaison plane. The Baker-two-five (WWII r/t phonetic nomenclature) was at Versailles, Ohio and, except for one brief period of activity, had been sitting there, tied down outside, for 14 years. One engine was partially disassembled and all the operating systems were in the condition you would expect under the circumstances.

Ray declined to say what he paid for the airplane. He took a couple of AIs with him, and nephew Dean Cunningham to act as flight engineer, and they had one engine running within an hour. Another six days were invested in re-assembly of the other big Wright R-2600 Cyclone, and overhaul of the hydraulic and other systems. Then they flew the Mitchell to Lawton on a ferry permit.

By mid-1980, 4,000 man-hours had been invested in a complete restoration. Ray had logged about 60 hours in the bomber, and was preparing to pull both engines for overhaul. "We're going to install all the guns and return the airplane to its original configuration, the way it was when delivered to the Air Force in January, 1945.

"We know it went overseas in February, 1945," Ray continued, "and it returned to the United States in July that year; but so far we have not been able to learn where it went or which unit it served with. If you are going to write about it, please mention the serial number, 4450535. Maybe someone who flew it then will remember.

"We've painted and marked it as a machine flown by the 498th Bomb Squadron of the 345th Bomb Group, which was in the Southwest Pacific. There weren't many of the J models produced with the hard nose like this one," he added. "There is a very neat field repair to the fuselage which suggests the possibility of combat damage."

We asked if he would estimate the B-25's present value and he said he didn't know, but that it did not matter since it wasn't for sale. Ray also reminded us that the Mitchell was older than he.

We asked about fuel consumption and he said that it burns 150 gallons per hour at 2,000 rpm, truing-out at 245 mph at that setting. It is certified in the Limited category.

The Warbird people—and the antiquers—will go to great lengths to obtain the remains of an old airplane. Aviation writer Martin Caidin's Ju52 Luftwaffe transport was rescued from a weed patch in Ecuador where it had rested for years. Other Warbirds have come from other countries, but there are still restorable hulks to be found in the lower United States and Alaska.

For those who like a challenge, perhaps the best prize yet to be claimed as this is written is six P-38Hs and two B-17Es that made wheels-up landings on the Greenland icecap during the summer of 1942. Each of the B-17s, from the 341st Bomb Squadron, 97th Bomb Group, was leading a flight of three P-38s of the 1st Fighter Group across the North Atlantic to England when they were trapped by weather and ran out of fuel. All eight aircraft landed on the same level stretch of ice and apparently are still there. The crews were taken out by dog sled after being found by a B-24 search plane. The official Air Force report of the incident is in the files of the Simpson Research Center, Maxwell, AFB, Alabama, and it gives the location of the downed aircraft as 65 deg 20 min north; 45 deg 20 min west.

THE ANTIQUES AND CLASSICS

The antiquers were originally organized by Robert Taylor of Ottumwa, Iowa into the Antique Airplane Association, and the AAA is still their exclusive organization despite the growing Antique Division within the EAA. A lot of them, of course, belong to both the AAA and EAA.

The AAA held its annual fly-in on Ottumwa Municipal Airport back in the sixties and attendance almost rivalled that of the EAA fly-in at Rockford, Illinois. But scheduled air carried service at both airports was certainly one of the factors that dictated that both events be moved. (*Everyone* has to get out of the way of the airlines. Everything from runways to navaids are primarily designed and built for their benefit—with your money.) In any case, the EAA event outgrew the facilities at Rockford; and an unfortunate accident at Ottumwa (a spectator walked into a turning prop) hastened the AAA's exit from that site.

Taylor moved the AAA headquarters and annual fly-in to Blakesburg, Iowa and excluded the public, so that event has been limited ever since (Fig. 3-8).

Fig. 3-8. A WACO YKC of 1934 (L) and an OX-5 WACO 10 of 1928, photographed at the Antique Airplane Association annual fly-in. From 1930, the WACOs were identified by three-letter designators, the first letter denoting engine make and horsepower; the second letter for wing design, and the third letter model or type. There were a lot of them. "Y" was for the 225-hp Jacobs engine.

Fig. 3-9. A neat Piper PA-22 TriPacer. The TriPacers, with 125 to 165-hp, were produced 1952-1960.

The antiquers seem more nostalgia-oriented than the Warbird restorers. They are apt to turn up at fly-ins dressed in peg-top breeches and field boots. White silk scarves and pre-war leather helmets and goggles are common, and there isn't likely to a transponder or encoding altimeter among them. They like small grass strips, draft beer, and Texas chili. They are a great bunch; pure middle-class America.

They search the old barns and check small, out-of-the-way airports for the skeletons of ancient civilian airplanes, and they do come up with some rare birds indeed. Ever hear of a Crosley biplane? A Rose Parakeet? How about an American Eagle? We've seen them, looking like new, along with Fleets, Robins, Travel Airs, Monocoupes and Wacos.

The antiquers do not invest the astronomical sums demanded by Warbird projects, and a 1927 Spartan C-3 is a lot cheaper to fly than a P-51. Still, restorable antiques are, if anything, *harder* to find because civil aircraft production during the twenties and thirties was not high, and since the majority of those wings were wood and fabric and too often parked outside, relatively few have survived. Too many of them disappeared as did a Curtiss Jenny and Thomas Morse Scout we knew about. Owner George Pollard flew this pair of WWI surplus planes during the thirties, but took the wings off and parked them in his backyard to comply with the law during WWII when all private airplanes were grounded and supposed to be rendered non-flyable. Weather and the neighborhood children took their toll, and after the war George paid a junkman to haul away the remains. It is a typical story. The oldest antiques, the WWI airplanes, are few indeed, and it is believed that the survivors have all been restored by now.

The unrestored classics, those built during the later forties and early fifties, are fast becoming scarce because so many pilots have recognized the economic good sense of their operation for personal use. Anything built by Piper between 1946 and 1960, from the J-5 Cruiser to the PA-22 TriPacer, becomes more attractive every day for low cost private flying (Figs. 3-9 and 3-10). The Dacron covering and finishing systems, now actually less costly than the old Grade A cotton fabric, lasts at least as long as cotton, and can make an airplane like a Piper Vagabond a very desirable fun machine with a fuel consumption of less than four gallons per hour and minimum maintenance. These are basic, no-frills airplanes, but as Bill Lear once remarked, you never have to repair, replace or maintain anything you leave out.

The economic operation of the lightplanes of the forties and fifties is steadily driving up their prices, of course, but there are some still to be found with high-time engines and deteriorating fabric that are reasonably priced. Parts are still available for those little Continental and Lycoming engines (used); and if one is willing to tackle the re-cover job himself, the refurbishing costs are minimal. The lowest price you can get on re-covering, say, an Aeronca Champ, T-Craft or Cub is around $3,000 today, and then it may be poorly done. The materials for the job, including all the solvents, cement, filler, primer and finishing coats, cost somewhere between $500 and $800 (that's 1981 dollars), depending upon the system employed (there are four FAA-approved synthetic fabric/finish systems: Razorback fiberglass, and the Dacrons of Ceconite, Stits and Eonnex. TAB Book No. 2252, *How to Install and Finish Synthetic Aircraft Fabrics*, details the procedures and compares each of them. Also see *Aircraft Dope and Fabric*, TAB Book No. 2313). The FARs allow pilot/owners to re-cover and finish an ATC'd production airplane if they work under the supervision of a licensed aircraft mechanic, and that doesn't require the mechanic to be on the scene throughout the job. Pre-sewn "envelopes" are available at little extra cost for most fabric-covered lightplanes, and these eliminate much of the labor and head-scratching.

Classics or antiques with plywood-covered wings should be considered with caution. Glued joints do deteriorate, and trapped moisture rots wood, and a thorough inspection of the internal structure really isn't possible without opening up the wing. It is probably best to absorb what the FAA has to say on this subject in Advisory Circular 43.13-1A & 2, before buying an early Mooney or Bellanca or Fairchild PT-19, for example. Aircraft spruce is just as good as metal in an airframe, and in some ways better, when properly maintained. But the operative term here is *"properly maintained."*

FAA Advisory Circular 43.13-1A & 2 is available from the U.S. Government Printing Office, Washington, D.C. 20402, or (quicker) from the Aviation Maintenance Foundation, Box 739, Basin, Wyoming 82410. Although the FAA calls it a "circular," it is more than 400 pages in length and is an absolute necessity to anyone constructing a homebuilt or restoring any kind of airplane. Its title is *Aircraft Inspection and Repair*, and it spells out the acceptable methods and techniques—acceptable that is, to the FAA.

THE ULTRALIGHTS

Actually, ultralight aircraft have been around from the beginning. Man has been struggling into the air with a minimum of horsepower and a maximum of optimism in both homebuilt and

Fig. 3-10. Ever see a more striking Piper Pacer? The PA-20 Pacer was introduced in 1950 and 800 were built during the two years it was in production. A few were powered with the 115-hp 0-320, most had the 125-hp 0-290D. Today some are converting the more common TriPacer to the taildragging Pacer configuration.

commercially produced flying machines that date back at least to Santos Dumont's 1907 monoplane of 20-hp. But today's ultralights have a totally new dimension. Aerodynamically, they are far more efficient, while modern construction materials also add to performance.

There are two kinds of ultralights and the distinction between them is important. If the machine has a mechanical landing gear it is an *airplane* and subject to all the FARs that pertain to homebuilt airplanes and their operations. But if the operator's feet constitute the machine's landing gear, it is a *powered hang glider* and the FAA, at this writing, has nothing at all to do with it: no inspection, and no certification is required for either the machine or its pilot.

Up to now, that has worked fairly well, although the FAA admits that it is keeping a skeptical eye on the unlicensed segment and has been kicking around, within the FAA, some proposed regulation. It appears that the FAA has hoped that the foot-launched machines would turn out to be sort of a fad that would soon die out. However, the movement continues to grow and promises to be a significant factor in fun flying because of its low cost (assuming that it isn't regulated to death). Therefore, by the time this book gets into print it is a good bet that Uncle Friendly will have made some formal proposals concerning the regulation of the machines with the leather-soled landing gears.

It is inevitable, human nature being as it is. There are always some people who just can't stand a good thing. Already, a few have flown powered hang gliders coast-to-coast; have reached altitudes above 14,000 ft, operated from shopping center parking lots and buzzed packed footbal stadiums. These dimbulbs, only a few in number, of course, merely confirm that every sport has its show-offs. But it only takes a few of the hey-everybody-look-at-me types to get the attention of the FAA—and the public the FAA is charged with protecting. So, the rules are coming.

Down in Australia, where the powered hang gliders took off in significant numbers before the movement really got started in the United States, proponents of the sport anticipated all this and, in effect, wrote their own common-sense safety rules which the Australian counterpart of the FAA soon made official (with, undoubtedly, a bureaucratic sigh of relief). The main restrictions in that law are that powered hang gliders may not be operated above 300 ft AGL; may not fly at night, over populated areas, or within five kilometers of an airport. The law has worked well in Australia, and may well be the model for a similar FAR.

The spectre of impending regulation was the main concern of the responsible people in this sport, and the reason that they organized and then tucked under the wing of the EAA.

The powered hang gliders have come a long way from the flex-wing "kites" that gave birth to this sport back in the early seventies. Rigid-wing hang gliders such as the Easy Riser and the VJ-24 evolved from the fold-up types, and the addition of a small engine was the next natural step. Chainsaw and snowmobile engines have worked well, although a number of other engines in the 20-hp range are being used. Most consume about one gallon of gasoline per hour. Empty weights range between 120 and 160 lbs and all those we have seen are designed for quick assembly/disassembly for transportation between one's home and the flying sites.

The most advanced powered hang gliders, in kit form, sell for $3,500 including engine. Others range downward from there in price. If one works from a set of plans alone, and scrounges his materials, it is possible to get by for $1,000 or less. Only simple hand tools are required for assembly. Since these are all single-place craft, it is essential that one obtain instruction in their operation, and the best way to accomplish that is through association with an ultralight EAA chapter.

It seems to use that it would be better if the powered hang gliders were called "superlights," and leave the term "ultralight" to that class of airplanes weighing 500 lbs or less, because this class of lightplanes was referred to as "ultralights" long before the powered hang gliders appeared.

Nomenclature aside, it is reasonable to expect that the ultralight *airplanes* will proliferate at a greater rate than the powered hang gliders during th eighties because of their greater utility and because the ever-increasing cost of flying even the smallest commercially-built airplane will point a lot of sport pilots toward homebuilts. A commercially-produced ultralight airplane is highly unlikely despite the obvious market for such craft. It is doubtful that a commercial product could be offered for less than $12-15,000, and the start-up costs of production, including the expensive process of obtaining an Approved Type Certificate from the FAA, would mean a very large investment in a market that the light airframe manufacturers would prefer to see disappear. Their profits are in the well-equipped four-placers and larger, that sell for $50,000 and up; and the main reason that they bother with two-place trainers at half that price is because they believe that "product loyalty" is an important sales factor and that all those new people coming into aviation are prone to buy the same brand of airplane they start out with.

The general aviation marketplace has followed the general economic patterns around the world for the last half century, modified only by government regulation in each country. Back in the mid-twenties, while the U.S. Federal Government ignored private aviation, except for legislation designed to impose responsibility on the barnstormers and develop the air mail routes, the British government was actively promoting private flying, especially ultralight airplanes, aided by the great London newspapers.

Beginning in 1923, an ultralight airplane competition was held at Lympne Aerodrome, sponsored by the Daily Mail, offering cash prizes for the best designs. The rules limited each entrant to single-place with an engine of no more than 45.75 cubic inch displacement (the 65-hp Continental that powered most J-3 Cubs had 171 cu. in.). Therefore, the airplanes at Lympne were fitted with engines that developed no more than 20-hp. Two, the English Electric Company's Wren, and the Sayers-Handley Page HP 22, had engines of only 24.6 cu. in. which produced 10-hp at 3,000 rpm.

The Wren was a 232-lb (empty) high-wing monoplane with 150 sq/ft of wing area, while the HP 22's empty weight was 250 lbs and its wing area 157 sq/ft. These numbers resulted in wing loadings of 2.8 and 2.75 lbs sq/ft at 420 and 430 lbs gross respectively. Both aircraft cruised at 40 and landed at 25 mph. The two-cylinder opposed engine was made by the A.B.C. Company of Walton-on-Thames, which later offered the 34-hp Scorpion that was built in some numbers during the late twenties.

The Lympne competitions attracted more than 20 different entires each year with most of Britain's major aircraft manufacturers represented; but after the appearance of the DeHavilland Gipsy Moth (the British Empire's Piper Cub) in 1926, interest in the British ultralights began to dwindle, and the 34-hp Halton HAC-1 and HAC-2 were the only commercially-produced ultralights listed in the 1928 edition of Jane's All the World's Aircraft.

In Germany, the company that would later produce the WWII Messerschmitts, Bayerishe Flugzeugwerke, offered a very clean little two-place low-winger, the M-23, fitted with a 20-hp Mercedes-Benz opposed engine, and which had a top speed of 75 mph and an empty weight of 440 lbs. The German Klemm L-25 was similarly configured, with the same engine and matching performance.

Fig. 3-11. The Rand Robinson KR-1 single-place and KR-2 two-place craft are VW-powered and return exceptional performances due to clean design and modern materials.

France's most notable contributions to the ultralight field are the Druine Turbulent and Jodel Bebe, both Volkswagen-powered. In fact, the French should be given credit for leading the way with VW engines in airplanes, since the Turbulents were flying with Bug engines for twenty years before those little powerplants began to find acceptance in American homebuilts.

The U.S., of course, leads the world in ultralight airplane activity today. Taking advantage of new materials and a number of good small engines, American designers have produced some ultralights with rather startling performances. Consider:

The single-place Rand-Robison KR-1 which appeared in 1972 pioneered in the use of rigid polyurethane shaped blocks covered with Dynel fabric to supplement a basic wooden airframe (Fig. 3-11). It has a retractable gear, is stressed to plus/minus seven Gs, and estimated cost of materials (1980 dollars) is $1,700 less engine and prop. Average building time is 800 hours. Fitted with a 60-hp VW engine this clean little 300-lb (empty) low-winger will cruise at 180 mph and land at 45 mph.

You think that is eye-opening? How about the Rutan VariEze which came along in 1975 with a simple "sandwich" construction of high-strength fiberglass, polyurethane foam and epoxy (Fig. 3-12). This two-place canard (tail first) has an empty weight of 490 lbs, a top speed of 208 mph and an initial climb-rate of 1,800 fpm. It is powered with the Continental 0-200 or Lycoming 0-235 (100-115 hp), which means a normal fuel consumption of about four and a-half gallons per hour. [*Editor's note*: for more details, see the author's own *Complete Guide to Rutan Homebuilt Aircraft*, TAB Book No. 2310.]

Then there is the single-place Taylor Mini-Imp (Fig. 3-13) designed for the 1700-cc VW engine (but which will accept a number of engines up to 115-hp). The Mini-Imp ("Imp" for "independently made plane") features simplified all-metal construction and is a pusher design resembling Ed Lesher's larger Teal (Fig. 3-14). It weights 520 lbs empty, which puts it over the arbitrary dividing line between ultralights and other airplanes, but there are several good designs in this weight class and who wants to complicate things by adding a semi-ultralight category? The Mini-Imp cruises at 150 mph, lands at 43 mph and has an initial climb rate of 1,200 fpm. Like the VariEze and KR-1, it is a proven design.

By the time this reaches print, designer-builder Molt Taylor should have completed all tests on the Taylor Micro-Imp, and it is something new. The Micro is basically constructed of—we hope you're ready for this—glass-reinforced *paper*. This greatly simplifies construction because this material is easily cut, shaped, drilled, riveted, bonded, sawn, sheared and finished. Taylor plans

Fig. 3-12. A seemingly-endless line of VariEzes; a total of 61 were registered at the 1980 Oshkosh show. There is no way to count the number currently under construction.

Fig. 3-13. Molt Taylor's Mini-Imp is single-place, has folding wings, and is designed for any engine between 60 and 115 hp. This prototype is fitted with a 60-hp VW, and cruises at 150 mph.

to offer a kit in which all the parts will be printed full size on the basic construction paper. The engine will be the Citroen 2CV de-rated to 25-hp. The prototype is presently in test, and Taylor hopes to market the kit for $3,000.

If you care less about speed and more about the relaxed pleasures of open cockpit flying, Gary Watson's Windwagon or the

Fig. 3-14. Ed Lesher's Teal has its 100-hp engine buried in the fuselage; propeller behind tail. Ed is an early EAA member.

Pober Pixie are two of the proven possibilities. Windwagon is a 230-lb all-metal low-wing monoplane powered by *half* of a VW engine producing about 30-hp. Construction costs run about $1,200, and, except for pop-riveter equipment, only simple hand tools are needed. Top speed is 100 mph, and Windwagon will cruise at 90 mph on less than two gallons of fuel per hour.

Paul Poberezny designed the Pixie, a parasol monoplane that may be described as a modern version of the Pietenpol Air Camper or Corben Baby Ace. Pixie employs conventional materials and construction methods—welded steel tube fuselage, wooden wings, fabric covering—and is powered by a VW engine of 60-hp. The single-place Pixie cruises at 85 mph, lands at 30, and is a joy to fly. Estimated cost of materials is $5,000, with building time averaging between 1,200 and 1,500 horus.

The 100-hp W.A.R. Replicas, scaled-down Corsairs, FW190s, etc., are in this same weight class, and are built up of a basic wood structure contoured with foam blocks and fabric-covered (Fig. 3-15).

Perhaps the most startling (and certainly one of the most successful) of the true ultralights is another Burt Rutan design, the single-place Quickie (Fig. 3-16). Can you believe 120 mph on 18-hp? That is just one of the reasons the 240-lb Quickie won the EAA Outstanding New Design Award in 1978. It gets 85 miles per gallon at a 100-mph cruise. *That*, my fellow aeronauts, is *efficiency*. Combine efficiency and performance with honest handling charac-

Fig. 3-15. The 100-hp W.A.R. replica Corsairs are built up of a basic wood substructure contoured with foam and covered with fabric. Half-scale FW190 was first of series and P-47 replica was seen at Oshkosh '80. Sea Fury and others are under development.

Fig. 3-16. A trio of Quickies. Note the fake wind-up key atop the machine at right. Of composite construction, the Quickie has a cruise of 121 mph—on 18-hp

teristics in an airplane that is easy and fun to fly, and you've got a winner.

Quickie construction is the sandwich type, using fiberglass over a foam core, and no special tools are required. Average building time from the kit should run about 600 hours and the current kit price is $3,000, which one may buy incrementally. Plans alone are $150. Quickie's engine is the Onan, more than a million of which have been produced for recreational vehicle generators and similar applications.

We should make it clear that, while the VariEze and other Rutan designs are marketed by the Rutan Aircraft Factory at Mojave, California, the Quickie kit or plans are sold by the Quickie Aircraft Corporation at Mojave.

The ultralights mentioned here represent just a few of the many good designs available in kit form or which may be built from plans.

4

A Show Plane Flies To Oshkosh

A large number of Oshkosh visitors fly themselves from the West Coast, and that's not too surprising when you consider what a high percentage of aviation activity takes place near the Pacific Ocean.

Jim Osborne, owner of the Stolp Starduster Corp. on the Flabob Airport in Riverside, California, has flown himself to Oshkosh on six different occasions (Fig. 4-1). Each trip has been with an exhibition sports biplane, either the single-seat Acroduster I that Osborne designed, or the Acroduster Too, a two-holer with a 260-hp engine.

Osborne's trips have been anything but routine. For the 1980 show, he headed out in a single-place model, NSA50X, with no radio, but that's not too uncommon for Jim. He seems to get there and back without nav/com. On this particular trip, he had the nav (VOR) coming home, but no com.

Jim started out from Flabob on a hot, smoggy summer day, just four days before the start of Oshkosh. His motorhome was already in transit with Shop Foreman Bill Clouse at the controls and would park in the exhibitor area as a home-away-from-home. He flew a "buddy system" on the trip east with John Helton, Riverside EAA member, and his 18-year-old daughter Janet flying the Acroduster Too, SA50X.

Janet Helton is the young lady who soloed the Acroduster Too and 35 other aircraft at Flabob on her 16th birthday. At the time of this cross-country trip, she had accumulated about 75 hours in the ship, according to Jim's best estimates. Janet did the flying and her father John handled the navigation (Fig. 4-2). The "Too holer" had a

Fig. 4-1. L to R: Janet Helton, Jim Osborne, Ed Boze, Harry Barr and John Helton.

complete nav/com system, and Jim used hand signals at close-range formation if he wanted to communicate en-route. Primitive, true—but effective.

The two Acrodusters flew formation for the entire trip. They circled up out of the smog, climbed through Cajon Pass and looked at the growing thunderstorms blocking the airways to Las Vegas, Nevada. First stop for fuel and a check to make sure that all systems were "go" was at the no-radio airport at Boulder City, Nevada (Fig. 4-3). Jim's Acroduster is an unlimited aerobatic competitor with a 180-hp Lycoming and Hartzell constant speed aerobatic prop—and no electrical system. Its rate of climb is spectacular, from brake release to 3,000′ in *80 seconds!* Indicated cruise is 160 mph at 2400 rpm and 24″ of mercury, but the power-off stalling speed is "around" 75 mph, so it really isn't the best machine in the world for an off-field landing.

After topping both Acrodusters at Boulder City, the trio headed on toward Page, Arizona (Figs. 4-4 and 4-5). This route parallels the Colorado River and the Grand Canyon (Fig. 4-6). It is spectacular scenery from any altitude, and even greater when you're getting down toward the surface of his high desert.

At Page, the trio met Bruce Aiken, a local charter pilot for the FBO, who was building an Acroduster. It was the first time that Aiken had ever seen a completed model, so there was much

79

Fig. 4-2. The Heltons, father and daughter in the Acroduster Too, with 18-year old Janet flying, father John navigating from the front cockpit.

looking, tire-kicking and question-answering. With a sports biplane, *any* fuel stop tends to become a hangar-flying session.

Out of Page, the two little biplanes headed up river over the spectacular scenery of Lake Powell and the red granite cliffs that contrast with the deep blue water of the Lake. Jim moved in close while John Helton shot pictures of the one-holer with an inexpen-

Fig. 4-3. First stop, Boulder City, Nevada; the Too waits its turn at the gas pumps.

Fig. 4-4. Jim Osborne in the single-place Acroduster off the right wing of the Acroduster Too. The two planes flew from California to Oshkosh together.

sive import Yashika 35mm camera equipped with a normal lens. To get the tiny Acroduster in this close for a picture takes some *mighty* familiar formation flying. Jim won't admit it, but perhaps the reason for photos in this area is because there's absolutely no place to make a forced landing along this part of the route (Figs. 4-7 and

Fig. 4-5. Below the sandstone cliffs over Glen Canyon, Arizona the two planes tuck in close.

Fig. 4-6. The Grand Canyon from below the rim; it's a mighty big ditch.

4-8). And that 75-mph touchdown speed must be taken into consideration.

Next stop was Montrose, Colorado, where the altitude is 5759 feet. That makes for "hot" landings with the little biplanes, but the main runway is 8500 feet long, so there was "no sweat," except that Jim's engine quit on roll-out because of a too-rich mixture, and the Heltons had to taxi back and give him a "prop." The one-holer

Fig. 4-7. Beautiful scenery, but no place to land down there.

Fig. 4-8. Through the windshield of the Acroduster Too over Glen Canyon.

has no electrical system. When Jim is flying alone, he uses a scrap piece of rope to tie the ship to a fence and has a glider tow hook on his tailwheel so he can prop the "bipe" safely, climb aboard, pull the chain and go flying.

It was time to call it a day at Montrose. Charlie West and Dave Karl shuttled twins in their hangar to put the two biplanes out of the weather and scrounged a car for the ride to town. "Every place we stopped with the biplanes, we met the nicest people," commented Osborne.

Next morning, the two little biplanes headed East over the top of the Rocky Mountains. It was cold at 12,455 feet (remember, you can't fly above 12,500 without a transponder except in those rare areas where the terrain goes to within 2500 feet of that altitude). In the Rockies, there is considerable of this terrain, so perhaps 30 minutes of the trip was approaching a bitter-cold 13,500 feet. The super VFR view was great, something that few people ever see from an open biplane (Fig. 4-9).

Next stop was Arapahoe County Airport near Denver where John Helton handled the radio contacts for a "flight of two." Here the altitude is a *mere* 5860 feet, making it a legal part of "the mile-high city." There was a driving rainstorm near Boulder, Colorado, and Jim flew a tight wingtip formation for landing. The broad windshield and top wing of the Acroduster I make the cockpit fairly dry—*until* you come to a stop and shut down the engine.

Then it was East and downhill all the way to McCook, Nebraska, where the altitude is 2579 feet and the outside temperatures were warmer than over the Rockies (Fig. 4-10). Here the trio met J. W. Johnson, son of FBO Melton Johnson, whose specialty is P-51 work. He has three hangars full of engines and parts and has built a flying wing sailplane. Johnson was yet another of the interested aviation buffs who looked at the two biplanes and went out of his way to show the visitors around.

Then followed a stop at Lincoln, Nebraska, where Harry Barr and Ed Boze who run Duncan Aviation compared notes. They had built an Acroduster I.

Over the rolling farms to the east, the two Acrodusters went on to Mason City, Iowa for another night's stop. When he shut down for the night, Osborne neglected to push his mixture control full forward and the pressure carburetor jammed. Early the next morning, there was no starting the one-holer, so mechanic Dan Neusbrough crawled under the cowl and soon had the problem fixed. Again, FBO Jerry Dyer had shuffled executive twins around to make hangar space for the two biplanes. He wouldn't take any money for the hangar, just a picture of each of the two biplanes.

The two continued on to Oshkosh, handling the traffic pattern daisy chain as a flight of two. They landed at 10:30 a.m. on a Friday morning, early enough to establish a good parking spot on the

Fig. 4-9. At 10,000 ft above sea level— and 50 ft above the surface—crossing the Rockies.

Fig. 4-10. The Colorado Badlands deserve their name.

display line for the Acroduster I. The two-holer went on to Fond du Lac, Wisconsin, where members of the Italian aerobatic team tested it for possible use in the International aerobatic competition.

After a week of talking and selling, running a clinic on Acroduster building, looking at other homebuilders' models and admiring the daily airshows, it was time for Osborne to drive to Fond du Lac and work with the aerobatic team for another week. Then it was time to go west again and take care of the aircraft parts store in Riverside.

Jim returned alone with the Acroduster Too. In the rush of getting away, no one could find a flying helmet with a headset that was operative, so Jim took off with plenty of navigation equipment but no capability of *listening* to anyone. There's something about Murphy's Law here (and it came home to bite Jim later in the trip), but there's nothing illegal, immoral or fattening about flying cross-country with no radio reception—just as long as you stay off airways and away from control-towered landing fields.

After a late start, Jim spent his first night at Prairie de Chien, Wisconsin, a delightful town at the confluence of the Wisconsin and Mississippi Rivers (Fig. 4-11). With 122.8 Unicom only, Jim had no need for his communications unit. The one thing that impressed Jim most about Prairie de Chein was that he could receive a different TV station, and get a good signal, on *every* channel in his motel room set.

The next day, he continued on to fuel at Audubon, Iowa, into a "helluva headwind—over 30 mph." Next stop was Seward, Nebraska, best known as the hometown of aviation writer/photographer Budd Davisson. Airport Commissioner Lyle Gamoe, former Chief of Police, told Jim that the town was looking for a new, energetic FBO, but Osborne declined the job suggestion.

Next fuel stop was at the Meadowlake Airport near Colorado Springs, an airport that isn't listed on many directories, where Jim estimated the runway to be "about ten feet wide." But that was ample for the Acroduster Too, despite a stall speed of 70 mph with comparatively sharp stall and sensitive control response. Osborne's brochure on the Too cautions, "An experienced taildragger pilot will have no trouble flying the Acroduster Too, but should get both cockpit and taxi time to acquaint himself with the airplane before takeoff. I recommend that a pilot without taildragger time obtain dual in something like a Cessna 140 or Starduster Too."

Weather over the Rockies was deteriorating, but Jim headed for Monarch Pass after a call to the FAA/FSS to take a look and see if he could get by underneath and into Montrose again. There was a more-or-less legal gap, and Osborne headed down the highway toward Montrose where he flew the pattern at a minimum altitude before landing in a rain and hailstorm. And it was wet again when he taxied to a stop.

Fig. 4-11. Shelia Hackett, the FBO at Prairie du Chien, Wisconsin, and the Acroduster Too.

Again the Montrose hospitality was super. He caught a ride uptown after the two-holer was safely in the hangar with Airport Manager and Fire Station operator Kim Carling, who wanted to build a Starduster or Acroduster II. Naturally Jim sent him the brochures on his return.

The next morning, Jim planned an early takeoff before the cumulus clouds began blossoming over the high country. He hoped for a straight line flight back to Page, AZ. Montrose is on the Denver Sectional and Page is on the Las Vegas Sectional, so Jim had both charts in the cockpit. He also had the VOR tuned for Montrose, but still had no communications capability.

Osborne was less than 40 miles west of Montrose when he began deviating to the north around the growing clouds. About 100 miles out, he ran out of the tailbearing from the Montrose VOR and reached for the Las Vegas Sectional. No such luck! The chart had slipped behind his seat and was lying somewhere in the tailcone of the two holer, far out of reach. There is a one-inch space between the seat and the side of the fuselage where the chart slipped through. "I should have been sitting on it," said Jim in retrospect. "The same sort of thing happened to me once before when I lost both the canopy and my maps with a two-placer." Thus he had neither a VOR frequency he could tune nor a chart with visual check points.

"I was pretty well lost," Osborne admitted. "The country out there is both lonesome and rugged, so an off-airport landing would have been a problem. However, I had plenty of fuel, and in that situation you're never *really* lost."

Using the self-preservation instincts of a long line of older pilots, Jim sized up his dilemma and picked up as much of a westerly heading as the weather would permit. When he came to his first big river, he turned left and downstream. That river led to a larger river that eventually led to beautiful Lake Powell. And at the downstream west end of Lake Powell is Page, Arizona, and its fine airport. He had been in the air almost two hours and still had an hour of fuel remaining.

Jim stopped to refuel, and "I got me another map." Then he headed down the Colorado River gorge. Since he was alone and way out from any civilization, he was almost compelled to go down into the canyon for a good look. After all, that big 260-hp Lycoming had been purring smoothly all the way to Oshkosh, through the Italian evaluation of the aerobatic competition, and all the way home. So down into the canyon he went and stayed there part of the

Fig. 4-12. The single place Acroduster (above) has a roll rate of 240 degrees per second and cruises at 165 mph. Engine is the Lycoming IO-360, and empty weight is 740 lbs. The two-place Acroduster Too is 260 lbs heavier, has more wing area, same engine, and is five mph slower.

way to Las Vegas. With cumulus building again over the desert, Jim reports that it was nice down in the canyon.

There was a thunderstorm over the airport at Boulder City near Las Vegas, but Jim was less than 200 miles from home—that was only a minor problem, and Jim had been gone for nearly three weeks. So with a full tank of fuel and a 170-mph cruising speed, it was just over an hour before Osborne was agitating the smog particles in the traffic pattern of Flabob, one of the few airports in the Los Angles Basin where no radios are required. Total flight time, round trip, was just under 30 hours.

Osborne began flying in 1939 and ran out of time and money. He began again in 1969 and has logged somewhere over 900 hours. All of his long cross-country flights have been on the way to Oshkosh, and all in a biplane. Next year at Oshkosh—with another biplane (Fig. 4-12), of course!

5

First Trip To Oshkosh

When you fly into the EAA Oshkosh show for the first time, you're too busy following instructions and watching out for other traffic to appreciate the magnitude of the show. Only after you're safely on the ground, tied down and registered do you begin to find out just how big Oshkosh really *is*. Then it takes a photo trip in the EAA helicopter to begin to get the feel of this annual affair (Fig. 5-1).

Oshkosh is now the largest single collection of airplanes, pilots and spectators watching an airshow ever to take place (Fig. 5-2). More than 10,000 airplanes and almost a quarter of a million people were in attendance for the first weekend of Oshkosh 1980. Managers of the show expect even bigger and better years to come.

When you fly over this mass of aircraft and sea of spectators, you feel like a mighty small part of a mighty big presentation. Yet there's a story to tell concerning every airplane in attendance.

We'd been wanting to go to the Oshkosh Fly-in for many years. A year ago we almost made it when a new Citabria was ready to pick up for a West Coast delivery the week of Oshkosh, but the new owner had plans of his own and we met the steady stream of pilots headed for Oshkosh at fuel stops like Worthington, Minnesota, Liberal, Kansas and Albuquerque, New Mexico, as we headed west.

Follow-up hangar-flying sessions with those who "made it to Oshkosh" convinced us that we wouldn't wait any longer, so the calendar was blocked off. As the first of August approached, our venerable 1952 Cessna 170B had its oil screens checked and new

Fig. 5-1. Record crowd on Sunday, as seen from the EAA helicopter. The main airshow runway, #18, is at the right of the photo. lake Winnegabo is at the top of the photo. All the aircraft in the foreground are classics on display.

oil added, the plugs were pulled and checked, and we put on a set of new tires. The back seat came out to make space for tent and sleeping bags that we hoped *not* to have to use.

FLYING EAST

Oshkosh begins officially on the first Saturday in August and runs for a full week, so we elected to fly out of the busy Los Angeles basin on Wednesday after work. As we drove to the airport through the smog, we could see billowing cumulus growing over the Sierra Madres. It would be a rough ride, we speculated—and it was!

We had planned a short hop to Dinosaur City on the old Interstate 66 because both a motel and cafe adjoin the packed-dirt, 3972' airport, elevation 5386'. This overnight spot would assure an early takeoff to put most of the 1650-mile cross-country junket out of the way on Thursday.

After climbing out of the smog at the Cable Airport where we base, we flew through Cajon Pass and had a nose-to-nose view of some of nature's wonderful desert thunderstorms. Las Vegas Flight Watch was reporting a thunderstorm to 35,000 feet over the field with winds up to 50 knots, rain and occasional hail. Eastward toward Needles and our proposed overnight stop, things didn't look much better. When Flight Watch called back and asked for our intentions, we advised that we were having a cockpit conference before deciding. It was either go back home, spend the night at a hot Apple Valley or an even hotter Daggett, or take a "chicken look" down Highway I-40 toward Needles. We throttled back to compensate for the turbulence and picked our way between the thunderstorms and the R-2501 restricted area. Eventually, the bone-dry desert town of Needles came in view with a cloudburst gushing from the skies above and lightning zapping cloud-to-ground. We crossed into Arizona, still uncertain of making Dinosaur City, but eventually Kingman came into view, and we soon landed next to the comfortable, reasonable fly-in motel along the old U. S. 40 (Fig. 5-3).

There's a gas pump marked "100 octane" at the truck stop gas station, but no av/gas. There's just too little fly-in traffic to justify the investment in an 8000-gallon tank of 100 octane, and distributors no longer handle partial loads to outlying airports. Luckily, we had ample fuel to overfly Grand Canyon the next morning and stop off at Page, Arizona.

No sooner had we parked at Page than Burt Rutan showed up with his twin-engine Defiant (Fig. 5-4). Mike and Sally Melvill

Fig. 5-2. Oshkosh from the air on a record day. Homebuilt and airshow aircraft are parked in front of the tower. Permanent buildings at the right house display booths. The "Fly Market" is in the foreground. Photo from an EAA helicopter.

Fig. 5-3. Author's Cessna 170B parked in the tiedown area at Grand Canyon Caverns, Arizona. Motel and cafe here ajoin a good 3972' flight strip. Underground caverns are near the motel. This was the first stop on the trip to Oshkosh from Southern California.

were tucked in next to him in their VariViggen (Fig. 5-5) on a two-plane fly-by—practicing for Oshkosh, of course. Burt, Mike, and Sally are old friends, having been of invaluable aid in the preparation of our recently published *Complete Guide to Rutan Homebuilt Aircraft* (TAB Book No. 2310).

A steering link on the Defiant's nose gear broke during Rutan's landing roll and Burt and Mike went to work on repairs (Fig. 5-6) while we filed with the FAA for a VFR flight along the inspiring scenery of Lake Powell toward Grand Junction, Colorado. At Page, 100 octane was $1.86, the highest we paid on the entire trip. Weather was good all the way as we followed the red sandstone cliffs and deep blue water of the Colorado River and picturesque Lake Powell, backed up for more than 200 miles behind the Glen Canyon Dam.

As Lake Powell drifted behind us, we picked up Grand Junction on the ADF and debated overflying it for a straight shot to Denver. Eliminating one stop would put us farther East, so we extended our flight plan to three hours and twenty minutes for Jeffco (Jefferson County Airport), just northwest of Denver.

It's hard to decide which scenery is more spectacular—the contrasting colors of Lake Powell or the granite grandeur of the Rockies at Vail, Colorado, over Interstate 30. It's all awe-inspiring scenery when viewed from a lightplane in respectable weather. We climbed to 12,500 feet for clearance over the 11,990-foot Loveland Pass highway tunnel just east of Vail and started our long descent into the Great Plains that begin at Denver.

AOPA's Airport Directory doesn't list a cafe at any general aviation airport in the Denver area. Stapleton International has all the amenities, but it is time-consuming to get into a busy jetport, fuel up, and catch a ride to and from the main terminal for lunch. "Jeffco" listed a "snack bar" at Aircraft Co., the Beech dealer, which was really a machine food dispenser with a couple of tables. The machines were almost empty, and the FBO took pity on us and drove us a couple of miles to a Safeway Market delicatessen while one of their linemen did the daily banking. The sandwiches were both ample and reasonable.

Weather continued good to the east, and since we were now over the mountains, it was literally downhill all the way to Oshkosh. We headed east with no definite destination in mind. We could have made Oshkosh after dark, but it would have been one helluva long trip in a fixed-gear, 135 mph four-placer, even with two pilots aboard. And, since we'd spent a good part of the day at altitudes up to 12,500', there was a fatigue factor to consider.

Fig. 5-4. Burt Rutan and Mike Melvill check a broken nose gear linkage on the twin-engine Defiant at Page, Arizona, with sandstone pillars showing in the background.

Fig. 5-5. Bound for Oshkosh, Mike and Sally Melvill climb out of their VariViggen after a non-stop flight from Mojave, California, to Page, Arizona. Nose of Burt Rutan's Defiant is in the foreground.

We picked Broken Bow, Nebraska as an overnight stop, mainly because the name was intriguing. The FAA FSS at North Platt had advised that Broken Bow didn't have 100 octane—but they were wrong. We had ample fuel aboard anyhow and taxied up to the neat office and hangar at Broken Bow just two hours and twenty-five minutes out of Denver. That was a total of seven hours for the day. The FBO, George Land, apologized because his loaner car had a broken fuel line, but he made a call to the Gateway Motel where the owner provided a ride without charge. A truck stop down the street had good food, and we called it a day.

ARRIVAL

Everyone we'd talked with in advance had said that the traffic jam at Oshkosh is a mind-boggling occurrence. One California pilot who had been there before said that he was going to arrive after midnight when there wasn't a long line of planes, but we decided that part of the personal experience of Oshkosh was to fly in with all the other troops. We did, however, stop at Baraboo, Wisconsin, some 20 minutes west of Oshkosh, to top off our tanks so that we wouldn't have to fuel at the super-busy EAA affair, especially not knowing procedures. As it turned out, fuel was available at Oshkosh from trucks.

Then came the parade into Oshkosh. We took off from Baraboo at 3:00 pm local time, climbed high enough to pick up the Oshkosh ATIS and reviewed the mailed-out sheet for the VFR arrivals to Oshkosh. This two-page briefing sheet was carried in the EAA magazine *Sport Aviation* and reprints were distributed to interested non-members.

Here's how it was detailed—and it did work well.

VFR ARRIVALS PROCEDURES

1. All inbound aircraft monitor the Oshkosh ATIS on 125.8 MHz when thirty-five miles out from Oshkosh. Be alert for arrival procedure in use.

2. See Graphic Notam for Fisk arrival routes and special instructions.

3. In light to moderate traffic situations, handling will be done in the normal manner. VFR check points and direct to the airport traffic patterns per tower instructions.

4. Special arrival procedures will be used in heavy traffic conditions. See Graphic Notam for Fisk VFR arrival procedure.

During periods of heavy traffic (when indicated on ATIS), all inbound aircraft will use the Fisk Special Arrival Procedure. Proceed clear of the depicted high density traffic area at altitudes and speeds

Fig. 5-6. Repairs to the twin-engine Defiant took over an hour. Soon Burt Rutan and Mike Melvill were back in the air, over the picturesque Lake Powell and across the Continental Divide toward the Jeffco Airport near Denver.

appropriate to direction flown. As you approach the village of Ripon, Wisconsin, Oshkosh VORTAC 232 degree radial at 18 miles, call Oshkosh Tower on 120.7 MHz. Proceed inbound toward Fisk on the south side of the railroad track. Arrival controllers will provide specific instructions using your aircraft color and type. You will be given traffic to follow as you approach Fisk.

The route to Wittman Airport will be issued by controllers at Fisk. Landing sequences and clearance will be issued by Oshkosh Tower 118.5 MHz.

VFR HOLDING—BEFORE RIPON

Traffic enroute to Ripon will be advised on the arrival ATIS to note your present position, maintain VFR conditions, and circle the geographic spot on the ground that you are currently over. Do not proceed to Ripon until advised to do so on the ATIS frequency. The approximate length of anticipated delay will be included in the ATIS message. This delay will normally not exceed more than three to five minutes duration. You may expect a release to proceed toward Ripon and on to Oshkosh via the published arrival route on the ATIS frequency.

VFR HOLDING—AFTER RIPON

Traffic will be instructed to hold from over the village of Fisk with a left turn westbound to the north end of Rush Lake, then counter-clockwise around the lake, then back northeast bound on the northwest side of the railroad track. (Be alert for other traffic on the southeast side of the railroad track.) This pattern may be reduced by controllers. The pattern will be at 1000 AGL for traffic up to 110 mph and at 1500 feet AGL for those who need 130 mph and up.

For the safety of all, please use speeds and altitudes as appropriate for your aircraft in your transitions and holding.

Holding patterns will be monitored by arrival controllers and traffic will be released to proceed to the airport on 120.7 MHz from these patterns. Do not pass Fisk until approved by controllers.

The instructions were great and we followed them to the letter. However, when it is your first trip into a strange airport, there is considerable searching for landmarks. As Ripon came up over the nose, we began to see that the specks in the sky were *not* just bugs on the windshield. The FAA controllers did an outstanding job of keeping their cool as we converged on Ripon and established an in-trail pattern over the railroad tracks.

The railroad tracks from Ripon to Fisk are visible, but buried in the grass. The Oshkosh 232 radial does the same job, but requires some attention inside the cockpit when you'd really feel more comfortable looking outside all the time.

At Fisk, an approach controller with a rented trailer with two-way radio, a land telephone line to Oshkosh Tower, and binoculars provided additional instructions from Ripon to Fisk and sequencing (Fig. 5-7). "Just listen to the tower; they'll talk to you; go to the tower now on 118.5," explained the Fisk controller as we passed overhead.

Between Fisk and the airport, we had perhaps ten aircraft in sight ahead and an undetermined number behind us that we didn't worry about. Oshkosh Tower continued a rapid patter, mainly urging a close-in pattern with a base leg not east over Lake Winnebago. Most visitors complied. The ship immediately ahead of us—it looked like a Swift—seemed to have some difficulty in slowing to 110 mph and was making sort of an "S" out of himself. His base leg to Runway 27 was wide over the lake, so we turned just enough inside him to allow for the excellent slow-speed handling of our 170B. The tower never called us until we were perhaps 200 yards from touchdown.

"High-winger over the railroad tracks, clear to land. After rollout, turn left into the grass and follow the flagmen."

Until you've heard it and milled around in the traffic pattern at Oshkosh, it is hard to believe that all this is happening so fast. Aircheck tapes have been prepared and played later at many pilots' meetings. Instructions come so fast and so steadily that the first-time listener usually says, "You've gotta be kidding. That tape has been edited and compressed." Not so, it's all for real!

We touched down and cleared the bustling runway, following the daisy chain of brightly painted aircraft toward an immense parking area at the west end of the field.

The EAA briefing sheet that carried the approach instructions also advised what to expect on landing. It read as follows:

SPECIAL NOTICE

Runways 4/22 and 13/31 will be closed to landings and takeoffs at least seven days prior to and throughout the EAA Convention.

All light single and multi-engine aircraft will be required to exit runways, taxi and park on grass areas of the airport. Hazard areas will be marked by cones and/or flags. Pilots are cautioned to be alert for, and remain clear of all marked areas. Pilots should exercise caution in operating aircraft on unimproved or grass areas due to rough ground and signs.

Aircraft arriving during the hours of darkness must park at the north ramp (hard surfaced) until daylight the following day. Pilots are responsible for moving their aircraft to an appropriate grass parking area before noon of the day following their arrival. Limited overnight tiedown space is available at the FBO for a nominal charge.

Pilots of large or heavy aircraft requiring hard surfaced area parking are required to make prior arrangements with the Airport Manager, Wittman Field Airport.

Soon one of the flagmen picked us out of the line and waved us down a diagonal taxiway toward the tower. Since this was closer to the center of things, we didn't object. Soon, there was another waveoff to a grass area (Figs. 5-8, and 5-9) with two signs saying "Classics, Display Aircraft" and "Classics, Camping."

A bright-shirted EAA man walked up to the door and asked if we were going to camp out. We told him "no." He then asked for our EAA membership card and told us to follow a young man on a minibike (Fig. 5-10) across the grass to a parking spot in the Classics display area just under the tower, between a Piper Pacer from Dallas and a tri-tailed Bellanca from Oklahoma (Fig. 5-11).

We shut down the Lycoming and rolled out of the cockpit. There was nothing but praise for the slick air and ground handling here by the EAA troops. We soon figured out that our 1952

Fig. 5-7. FAA trailer at Fisk was used to direct traffic in trail before arrival at Oshkosh. FAA Controller Doug Radtke, Madison Wisconsin, had both two-way radio on the approach control frequency and a direct phone line to the tower. Patch on his shirt says "World's Busiest Air Traffic Controller."

Fig. 5-8. A parachute canopy and Cessna 195 wing serve as an ultralight tent for this family of five.

Fig. 5-9. Camp area for homebuilts and show planes. What is a Cessna 180 doing there? Well, many of us may not realize it, but the 180 has been in continuous production since 1953. Technically, the 1953 and '54 models are "classics."

taildragger was truly a Classic (built between January, 1946 December, 1955), so we filled out an entry form for the judging competition. We keep N2672D in good shape and had polished her laboriously before the Oshkosh trip. She has a year-and-a-half-old Imron paint job that we're kinda' proud of, as well as the 180-hp Lycoming conversion kit which doesn't spout oil. However, our good "transportation machine" was no match for some of the painstakingly restored classics. We spent many hours in the next week just walking through the rows upon rows of parked aircraft, admiring the TLC that made these truly showpiece airplanes. The first opportunity we had, we pulled out polishing rags and cleaner to take care of the buggy hitchhikers we had picked up enroute (Fig. 5-12).

After registering the 170B in the nearby booth (Fig. 5-13), we pulled out our six aluminum extrusions, each about four feet long, and pounded them into the rich earth under each wing and the tail. Then came heavy nylon rope and a durable set of aluminum chocks to complete the tiedown procedure. For those who had forgotten to bring tiedowns, the EAA had sets for sale at very reasonable prices. Several times during the ensuing week, we had reason to be glad that we'd brought solid tiedowns. Two days before the end of the 1980 show, a ferocious line of thunderstorms pummeled the

Fig. 5-10. Classic Cessna 140A taxiing on the grass near the plane camping area for EAA members only.

Fig. 5-11. A portion of the Classic Area at Oshkosh includes a Navion, Fairchild 24, Mooney Mite, Luscombe, Ercoupe and a passel of Pipers identifiable from the air. Arrow indicates our Cessna 170B.

Fig. 5-12. Julia Downie applies a fresh coat of polish as the family 1952 Cessna 170B is tied down in the "Classic" display area. Note aluminum extrusions pounded into the ground for tiedowns. These stakes held securely despite heavy rains and winds up to 60 mph during the week-plus program.

Fig. 5-13. Registration booths were set up near the main gate. Predictably, a goodly number of EAA memberships were issued at the beginning of the show.

Fig. 5-14. George Varga answers questions for visitors about his popular two-place "Kachina." Two versions of the Varga airplane were on display, but a new taildragger modification didn't make the show this year (1980) because of FAA "paperwork."

area, pulling loose almost half of the ultralights on display. Fortunately, our ship and our neighbors' didn't fly loose—and there was no hail to damage aluminum skins or fabric.

We signed in and picked up press credentials that would take us anywhere for the next week and pondered the most painless way to get our bags and cameras to the Motel 6 a mile from the airport, where we'd join George Varga (Fig. 5-14) and his Kachina troops from Chandler, Arizona. George was a day late bringing in his new 180-hp "Kachina" (Fig. 5-15) and was still sputtering because he was unable to get a last-minute ferry permit for the new taildragger version of his ship developed by Norm and Joyce Hibbard of Oakland, California. [*Editor's note: the taildragger Kachina has since been certified, as has the 180-hp engine for both taildragger and tri-gear variants.*

There's a standard fee for cabs in Oshkosh: $4.90 will take you anywhere in town, so we passed our gear over the storm fence around the parking area, loaded it into a cab, and were soon relaxing for the night, swapping flying "lies" with pilots from all over the country.

Fig. 5-15. Visitors mill around the ersatz R.A.F. paint job on the new 180-hp Varga "Kachina" at Oshkosh. Manufacturer George Varga ferried this two-placer in from Chandler, Arizona.

THE GREATEST AIR SHOW ON EARTH

The following week was challenging, fatiguing, inspiring—we never *did* see it all. We viewed innovative new designs, looked at petted and pampered originals and replicas of the oldies, and admired the Warbirds (but we didn't find a flying copy of the Curtis C-46 we once flew). We walked through the ultralights with respect for the intestinal fortitude of this new breed of intrepid airmen, but with just a bit of old-fashioned suspicion at some of the basic designs that still require weight shifting for control.

Aviation is usually a family affair—or the family usually breaks up. EAAers are even more closely knit because you can hardly share a garage or a front room with a three-year building project unless the wife is interested and/or compatible with airplanes. Thus, a great deal of effort goes into planning women's affairs at Oshkosh (Fig. 5-16). There's a Friendship tent sponsored by the Ninety Nines, the International Organization of Women Pilots. EAA women's forums are held daily. An emergency life-saving course (including cardiopulmonary resuscitation) is presented by the Winnebago County Auxilliary Police. "Operation Thirst" asks women visitors to help prepare sandwiches and soft drinks that are distributed to flight line EAA workers. Supplies for these snacks are donated by local businesses.

There's a pinch-hitter course for non-pilots. Clinics cover subjects ranging from craft sessions to free facials, how to make Christmas ornaments and macrame, "Storage Space that Works," "Chat with a Flight Instructor," and even "Creative Lunches and Snacks for Airplane Travel."

The EAA Oshkosh planners have anticipated just about every need for the visitor, including a Finance Department booth where personal checks can be cashed for EAA members; an emergency medical station (Fig. 5-17); a post office which furnishes a special post mark with an EAA Oshkosh logo (Fig. 5-18), and an International Hospitality Tent for the many foreign visitors, to mention just a few.

To assure the continuing excellence of this airshow, Paul and Tom Poberezney, with the aid of all the EAA workers, were assessing everything with an eye to next year's show and the expected increase in numbers. (We sent prints of the helicopter shots of the busiest day to Paul for future planning purposes.)

There's a hustle-bustle everywhere, but it isn't frantic. The events are planned far in advance and the programs seem to be

Fig. 5-16. Women's craft tent was only one of several centers planned to keep the ladies busy while the men plodded endless miles along the flight line, verbally "kicking tires" and admiring super craftmanship.

Fig. 5-17. Doctors are available at all hours. Most complaints involve blisters and headaches.

Fig. 5-18. The mobile post office on the field cancels stamps with a special postmark.

under complete control. While it isn't a rigid program, there's very little ad libbing (Fig. 5-19).

After your first visit, you don't tell your flying buddy, "I'll see you at Oshkosh" unless you have a specific time and location. The airport and surrounding campgrounds are just too big and there are just too many people to count on meeting. For example, we'd planned to have dinner with Irv and Cathy Culver, who were attending with their Turbo 210 (Fig. 5-20). Irv designed the Cosmic Wind Goodyear racers that were flown by Tony LeVier and Herman "Fish" Salmon shortly after WW II, and he designed the Lockheed Rigid Rotor helicopter, among other achievements. We would *never* have found them in the acres and acres of wing-to-wing aircraft in the camp-out area, had not Irv left a note for us in the AOPA booth (Fig. 5-21) giving the row and location of his airplane. We were able to get together.

Conversely, it is difficult to get from one presentation to another without stumbling into another pilot that you haven't seen for years. By the time you exchange words, you're probably late for the next presentation you wanted to take in—but that's all a part of Oshkosh.

Fig. 5-19. Near the main gate is a signboard outlining restrictions placed on visitors to the flight line at Oshkosh. Note that the flight line is accessable only to registered EAA members, guests of members, members of other aviation groups and licensed pilots.

Fig. 5-20. Irv and Cathy Culver, Playa del Rey, California, spent a full week camped on the flight line at Oshkosh, sleeping in the tent set up beside their Cessna T-210. Restrooms, cold showers and a grocery store were nearby.

Fig. 5-21. You have to like people to man one of these booths. Bob Warner, Vice President for AOPA, talks with potential members at the busy booth.

We toured the vendors' booths, seeing many new products that heretofore had been nothing more than advertisements (Fig. 5-22 through 5-26). And, of course, such window shopping can be expensive. We spent almost as much money as our two-way, 29-hour fuel bill on a new prefab "easy-to-install" upholstery kit for the 170B. This all started when we saw another 170B owned by Donald Fairbetter of Edmond, Oklahoma (Fig. 5-27). It was also in the Classic display area with a beautiful interior which the owner advised he had done himself with an Airtex upholstery kit. We spotted the Airtex booth in the Exhibit Hall and subsequently attended a workshop conducted by the owner, Don Stretch (Fig. 5-28). Finally convinced that we could install it ourselves, we fussed over colors for three days and finally utilized our Visa Card for side panels, carpeting and seat covers. Perhaps next year, with the new interior, we can come a bit closer to being a true classic—though our 180-hp modification keeps us out of "true classic" competition.

At the upholstery workshop, we met Aloha Good from St. Joseph, Missouri, who was attending many workshops, including welding and fiberglass, to learn techniques to help her husband in restoring older aircraft and repairing cars. Their visit was even

Fig. 5-22. The exibitors in the permanent buildings, more than 200, are kept busy in what is, in effect, the world's largest airplane store.

Fig. 5-23. Another building full of aviation exhibitors.

Fig. 5-24. Vendors' booths were busy from the 9 a.m. opening time until 4 p.m. when the air show started. It was wall-to-wall people, with even more jammed into the two permanent buildings when it was raining outside.

Fig. 5-25. A Pitts S-1 Special sport/aerobatic biplane partially assembled in the display area.

Fig. 5-26. Custom T-shirts are created on the spot in the South Exhibit Building. Mad Rags had five busy booths.

Fig. 5-27. Cessna 170B owner, Donald Fairbetter of Edmund, Oklahoma, left, proudly shows his new pre-fab interior to Don Stretch, Vice President of Airtex, the company who made up the upholstery kit.

Fig. 5-28. Don Stretch does his thing in demonstrating how his pre-fab upholstery kits work in the Airtex booth at Oshkosh. Facial expressions are interesting. This booth cost the authors the price of a new interior for their Cessna 170B.

more expensive than ours. Don Good bought a used tri-tail Bellanca and flew it home on a ferry permit (Fig. 5-29).

THE FLY MARKET

We went through the "Fly Market," EAA's answer to the corner Flea Market (Figs. 5-30 through 5-33). We were tempted by Arizona turquoise and coral, looked at sheet aluminum and extrusions, tiedown rope and rustic lawn furniture built near Oshkosh by a WWII fighter pilot. We purchased about three pounds of airborne "gorp," a clear plastic sack of nuts, bolts, washers, PK screws and very assorted bits and pieces that should be in every owner's airport locker or hangar.

A permanent EAA sales hangar was open daily, and from the number of new blue and white EAA ballcaps, jackets and T-shirts, they did a brisk business. Also for sale here were jewelry, decals, patches, shirts, postcards, model kits, flight bags, buckles, flying suits, technical publications and even cookbooks.

Food and vending machines were consigned to Zaug's of Appleton, Wisconsin. There were 21 outlets on the field ranging

Fig. 5-29. Don Good, St. Joseph, Missouri, hadn't planned to buy an airplane at Oshkosh, but this tri-tailed Bellanca caught his eye and he purchased it on the spot.

from sodas and snacks to cafes with full breakfast and dinner to a cafeteria (5:30 a.m. to 9:00 p.m.), to sandwich shops and fully-supplied stores for campers and tents. There was a special steak night and another night for a fish boil. Food was surprisingly good and reasonable for catered service.

Fig. 5-30. EAA "Fly Market," the Oshkosh version of a flea market, had just about anything available you might want to purchase from nuts and bolts to aviation memorabilia.

Fig. 5-31. Wanna buy a run-out engine or a set of used wheels and tires? You name it and it's for sale at the EAA Fly Market.

Fig. 5-32. You'll find just about everything, and just about every costume, in the Fly Market at Oshkosh. Classic Roadsters seem to interest pilots and homebuilders. They should—they're homebuilt kit cars. Note VW at left decked out as '40 Ford.

115

At Oshkosh in 1980, there was none of the feeling of gloom and doom that has permeated the aviation scene in recent times. Cessna did not exhibit at Oshkosh, but Piper, Beech, Mooney, Varga, and others were there. Every vendor and factory representative with whom we talked were enthusiastic. Homebuilt designers were selling all the plans they brought, and, like Burt Rutan with his Long-EZ, they were kicking themselves for not bringing more sets of plans.

Personal first impressions: Wake up and look out the window. It's raining, so snooze a little while and then click on the transcribed weather broadcast on the TV from a NOAA station in the area. It's going to clear shortly, so now is the time to get breakfast and get with it.

Dispite the drizzle, all roads to the airport are jammed. It takes a while to get to the main gate and we're glad that we already have EAA credentials to avoid the long lines at the ticket gates (Fig. 5-34). What's first? Go to the airplane and leave some gear in the cabin. Then head for a scheduled clinic presentation. Maps of the various activities are excellent and directional signs are good. We check the bulletin board in the Press Building for any messages

Fig. 5-33. The Fly Market, world's biggest aviation flea market is always a busy place.

Fig. 5-34. Oshkosh is people, thousands upon thousands of them. These are airplane people who plan vacations months in advance to coordinate with the early August date of the EAA show.

(Fig. 5-35). Then comes a sampling, once-over-lightly, of the display booths. Since this is out of the rain, we're jammed in with wall-to-wall people.

When the rain ceased, as predicted, most everyone goes outside to walk down the line upon lines of glistening display aircraft (Figs. 5-36 through 5-39). Paint, polish and fresh raindrops give the late-summer gathering almost a Christmas snowflake appearance. But that may be because we really like to look at unusual airplanes.

As soon as the weather comes up to VFR, a steady stream of arrivals circles the airport. This is a show within a show. Arrivals land on Runway 27 while local EAA fly-bys go off and land on Runway 18. Early in the morning before the winds come up, no-radio ultralights buzz around to the west of the north-south runway.

DAY TWO

On Sunday, the second day of the show, there wasn't an empty parking space in the grass surrounding Wittman Field. The entire transient aircraft camping area on both sides of Runway 9/27 was full. The show aircraft area was full. Classic, antique and

Fig. 5-35. One of several EAA personal message and swap announcement boards. Handy for locating a friend or trading an airplane.

Fig. 5-36. Burt Rutan's popular Long-EZ is pushed through the crowd after completing a non-stop flight to Oshkosh from San Francisco. Rutan is pushing on the left side of the canard wing while his father, Dr. George, pushed the right winglet. Burt's brother Dick made the record flight.

Fig. 5-37. Here's the scene along the flight line at Oshkosh. Runway 18 heads down to the right of this helicopter photo. Departures were routed at least a mile south of the field before turning on course.

Fig. 5-38. There are crowds everywhere. Here visitors watch air show performer Art Scholl, Rialto, California, as he has a problem starting his Super Chipmunk.

custom-built parking areas were jammed (Fig. 5-40). FBO's outside the area of the EAA program were also full. It was the biggest assembly of airplanes *anywhere*. From a helicopter, it was just *stupendous!*

After the full house the first weekend, some visitors departed. Alert flagmen, aided by up-to-date information from the EAA helicopter, marked these vacated spots and directed new arrivals to the vacancies. A surprisingly high percentage of hardy, dedicated afficionados braved the rain and heat, thunderstorms and early departures to spend a full week at Oshkosh.

The 4:00 p.m. to 7:00 p.m. airshow differed somewhat from day to day, but many of the performers presented a different program on different days. Warbirds of the WWII era performed along with the full program of the Confederate Air Force. Aerobatic teams included all the big names in the business; the Christen Eagles, flown by Charlie Hillard (Fig. 5-41), Gene Soucy and Tom Poberezny, presented a spectacular three-plane aerobatic ballet (Figs. 5-42 and 5-43). Montaine Mallet and Daniel Herigoin had their two-plane precision act, "The French Connection," honed so

Fig. 5-39. One of the bulletin boards (L) and film shop (R). This view is from the control tower. A powered sailplane, and what appears to be a Porterfield, remind us that of the more than 1,500 show planes down there, we have photographed only a fraction.

Fig. 5-40. Airplanes parked in the Classic camping area were wing-to-wing. The new Theater in the Woods area can be seen in the foreground, center, where programs were scheduled nightly.

fine that it was almost too close for comfort (Fig. 5-44). Duane Cole, Art Scholl (Fig. 5-45), Bob Herendeen, Bob and Pat Wagner—you name them and they were thre). The *extremely* noisy U.S. Marine Corps Hawker-Siddeley AV-8A Harrier opened the show with its gravity-defying vertical takeoff and landing presentation—and you had to close your ears. All in all, the professional performers were great, super-stupendous, and awe-inspiring. They put on one helluva show!

Oshkosh city buses and chartered buses, many from nearby shopping malls, carried people to and from the airport. Long lines of cars jammed roads going to the airport each morning—and on the weekend it was even *worse*. We lucked out by taking a free chartered bus sponsored by Copp's Department Store across the freeway from the Motel 6. The idea was to do your shopping at Copp's and haul the goodies back to your campsite. The local school bus driver knew a back way, far south of the regular entrance and cutting back along a narrow secondary road. Traffic control was directed as much as possible by the EAA helicopter working with EAA Security and local policemen. There were surprisingly few SNAFUs.

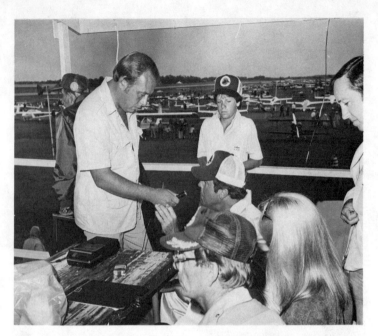

Fig. 5-41. Charlie Hillard (seated), leader of the Christen Eagle aerobatic team is interviewed at Oshkosh.

Fig. 5-42. The Christen Eagle team, Charlie Hillard, Tom Poberezny and Gene Soucy, perform with three Eagles at Oshkosh.

Fig. 5-43. The Christen Eagles aerobatic team flies their intricate aerial ballet in perfect formation with all eyes below turned skyward.

ENDURANCE TEST

The scope of the visitor's activities was strictly a function of the strength of legs and feet. For the first three days and nights, we

Fig. 5-44. Back-to-back precision, with no margin for error: Montaine Mallet and Daniel Heligoin, the "French Connection," in their CAP 10s.

nursed aching leg and feet muscles in the motel. After that, it seemed that they just went numb. People carried "Jiffy Seats," a three-cornered cane with a collapsible canvas seat in the middle; these were a popular sales item in the booth at $14.45. Many people walked with aluminum patio chairs hung over their arms (Fig. 5-46).

The EAA staff utilized their fleet of 26 VW Bugs, stripped of the doors and not licensed for highway use (Figs. 5-47 and 5-48). These radio-equipped Beetles had a go-everywhere capability and conspicuity that put EAA staffers in key positions with a minimum of strain.

Some of our time was spent resting feet and legs, stretched out under the wing of our Cessna with a blanket over the grass. However, there was little or no chance to sleep. Visitors stopped to talk about our ship or theirs. Then there was always an unusual fly-by or time for the airshow to commence. Yes, you could rest, but nobody comes to Oshkosh to sleep during daylight hours—and not *much* of the night, either.

What do you do at Oshkosh when you're not watching the daily late afternoon air show (Fig. 5-49) or camped on the flight line looking at fly-bys? There are so many scheduled activities that no single visit is going to touch all the bases. For example, the EAA scheduled two daily forums outlining EAA activities, the (EAA) Chapter and its designee, auto fuel, and EAA family activities.

Specialized workshops (Figs. 5-50 through 5-52) covered welding, woodworking, metal shop, synthetics, including fiberglass, foam and epoxies, a fabric shop, upholstery, a how-to-do-it on cutting, fitting, frilling and forming plexiglass, and several engine clinics. A special women's workshop covered aluminum and steel welding as well as fabric covering.

Daily youth programs were set up at the Camp Scholler area (Figs. 5-53 and 5-54) for softball, volleyball, jogging, horseshoes and table tennis, games, and special craft projects each day.

Special days are scheduled for each Oshkosh program. In 1980, one day's program was set aside "to honor those magnificent men and women and their flying machines" with General James Doolittle as honorary chairman for the day. E. M. "Matty" Laird, designer and builder of the Laird Super Solution, was present. Doolittle flew Laird's Super Solution to victory in the 1931 Bendix Air Race from Cleveland to Newark (Figs. 5-55 through 5-57). In these days before FAA, the construction of this racer was begun on

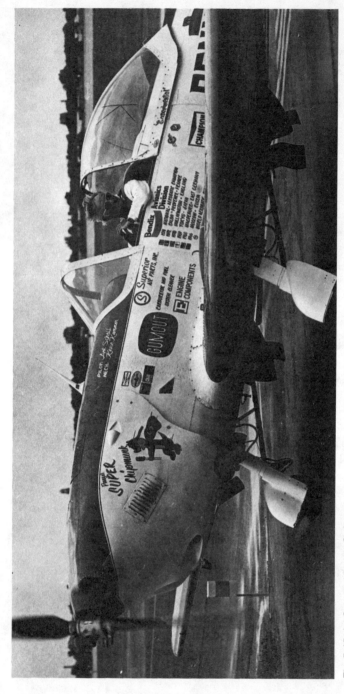

Fig. 5-45. Art Scholl of Rialto, California in his specially modified DeHavilland Chipmunk; another of America's top aerobatic pilots. Scholl has made several appearances on TV's "That's Incredible."

Fig. 5-46. Aluminum lawn chairs were carried by many EAAers who had been to the annual fly-in before.

Fig. 5-47. Paul Poberezny, President and Founder of the EAA, with one of the VW "Beetles" used to get around the mammoth airport at Oshkosh. His two-way radio call sign is (of course) "Red One."

Fig. 5-48. Tom Poberezny gives a flight-line interview to a TV crew. The EAA owns 26 open-cockpit VWs that are used by volunteers to keep things running smoothly on the ground.

Fig. 5-49. There is a lot happening above as well. During the first week in August, this is the busiest airport in the world.

Fig. 5-50. Men and women try their hand at fabric sewing during one of many EAA workshops. Homebuilders with families have been known to attempt to turn the fabric work over to their long-suffering wives.

Fig. 5-51. An overflow crowd at the Synthetics Workshop listened to Burt Rutan, Mojave, California, talk about composite aircraft design and fabrication.

Fig. 5-52. Ted Hendrickson conducted the propeller workshop.

Fig. 5-53. The Camp Scholler area is for motor homes and pickup campers.

130

Fig. 5-54. Wall-to-wall campers jam the Camp Scholler area. Many Oshkosh visitors—particularly those within a reasonable driving distance of the fly-in, find this the most practical way to go.

July 8th, and the airplane was ready for flight test on August 22nd—both in 1931.

An EAA "Schoolflight" display was available for viewing and talking about. Behind Workshop #2, a partially-completed Acro Sport II is being completed by students of the Messmer High School. An additional EAA Schoolflight booth was manned during the fly-in to help promote the concept of building airplanes in high schools. More than 366 schools have started programs and over 160 aircraft have been completed with the help of almost 1,000 EAA Tech Reps.

Seven tents are erected for scheduled programs from 9:00 a.m. to 4:00 p.m. daily and again after the air show for evening presentations (Fig. 5-58). Subjects range from theory of design, construction techniques and flight safety to government regulations and flapping wing flight. Each speaker donates his time, talent and know-how. In 1980, NASA had 14 different presentations, and AOPA had presentations ranging from instrument procedures to flying relaxed, and also coping with ATC (Fig. 5-59). An introductory pinch-hitter course was presented on four days, and aviation weather films were shown nightly.

The Fly Market was an interesting place to brouse, talk and perhaps haggle on a price. Sales were made from well-equipped tents or from a card table put up in front of a camper. The aviation enthusiast could find almost anything that his heart (and his pocketbook) might desire. Among the booths and vendors' displays in the Fly Market were offerings of memorabilia: WWII leather jackets with unit patches, wings of the various services, and even medals. There were a couple of Distinguished Flying Crosses (DFC) lying in a delapidated tray for sale, unemotionally, to whomever wanted this symbol of a Nation's respect—just for the exchange of cash. As one who stood at attention in a tea paddy in the rain in India to receive a DFC several wars ago, I found the offering obscene. I didn't have the curiosity to find out what the medals were selling for; perhaps I didn't want to know.

But all in all, the Fly Market offerings were interesting. Operators of the non-aviation-oriented booths here and in the Exhibit Halls commented candidly that they were there for the exposure to large crowds of people who had enough money to afford airplanes—or at least be interested in them. While many homebuilders, lightplane owners and just plain (plane?) aircraft buffs would discount the statement that pilots and owners have more than their share of money, it is an interesting—if in-accurate—concept.

A visit to the FAA Control Tower (Figs. 5-60 through 5-62) is a must for first-timers. It takes a bit of negotiation over the phone, and there's a conspicuous sign that reads, "Visits limited to 5 minutes, "but once you do get in the tower cab it's worth all the effort. Tower Chief Ryan F. Grove is aided by a long list of controllers brought in for the week from nearby facilities in Chicago, Cleveland, Minneapolis and others to beef up the regular seven-man staff at Oshkosh. The EAA program carries a complete list of FAA personnel, all of whom have volunteered for this assignment.

For those hardy souls who had the strength to go for more after dinner, there was dance music at Camp Scholler, a full evening of programs at the new Theater in the Woods, and featured motion pictures (Fig. 5-63). Evening speakers included Larry Newman, crewmember on the Atlantic Balloon "Double Eagle;" Bryan Allen, who made the first man-powered flight over the English Channel; author and lecturer Martin Caidin; John Baker, President of AOPA (Fig. 5-64) a musical presentation by the Young

Fig. 5-55. **August, 1931:** E.M. "Matty" Laird congratulates Jimmy Doolittle after Doolittle had flown from Burbank, California to Cleveland, Ohio to win the 1931 Bendix Trophy in the Laird Super Solution (courtesy E. M. Laird).

Fig. 5-56. **August, 1980**: Forty-nine years later, the same scene is unwittingly re-created at Oshkosh as Laird and Doolittle again congratulate one another. During the 1980 Oshkosh meeting, both designer Matty Laird and pilot General James Doolittle (in cockpit) were honored for their many contributions to avaition. Doolittle was Honarary Chairman of the event to honor "those magnificent men and women and their flying machines." One of the many pioneers who attended was T. Claude Ryan of San Diego, California.

Fig. 5-57. EAA's Museum replica of the Laird Super Solution, circa 1931, was wheeled into the "winner's circle" at Oshkosh to revisit the man who created her and the man who won with her—E. M. "Matty" Laird and Jimmy Doolittle.

Fig. 5-58. Exhibitors' tents made an excellent place to hide from approaching showers.

Fig. 5-59. There was standing room only in the tent where the Aircraft Owners and Pilots Association (AOPA) conducted a series of seminars.

Fig. 5-60. During the air show, the grass around the control tower is used as a resting place by leg-weary visitors. With the exception of eight controllers and the Chief regularly assigned to Oshkosh Tower, all other FAA personnel volunteer for this hectic assignment.

Fig. 5-61. FAA crew working heavy traffic from the Oshkosh Tower. Controllers from many facilities bid for this high-pressure job. Left to right are Karen Swanton, Muskegon, Michigan; Bob Margala, Madison, Wisconsin; and Lee Arenson, Janesville, Wisconsin.

Fig. 5-62. Permanent buildings and tents looking north from the control tower. The EAA Finance office is in the foreground. EAA members may cash out-of-state checks here.

Fig. 5-63. Theater in the Woods on a drizzly evening; a feature film every night.

Fig. 5-64. AOPA's John Baker imparts some good humored aeronautical wisdom to an after-supper crowd.

Americans, an awards banquet, an annual contest to pick Miss and Mrs. EAA, and much, much more (Fig. 5-65).

Flight-line admittance was limited to EAA members and their immediate families (Fig. 5-66). That's one reason that three EAA membership booths did a brisk business during the opening days of the show. This control limited spectators in the various aircraft parking areas and on the flight line to those who had some personal interest in airplanes in general and EAA in particular.

An excellent public address system stretched down the flight line. Interviews with designers, pilots, personalities and VIPs continued all day long (Fig. 5-67). The best of the airshow announcers took over at 4:00 p.m. daily to narrate the various flying demonstrations. The blaring of the PA system blended with the throaty roar of big round engines to create an atmosphere of sound that was, in itself, exciting.

Oshkosh planning is *not* a spur-of-the-moment affair. Trade show booths are booked *a full year* in advance. Commercial space in the aircraft area and the Fly Market has a similar lead time. Housing and car rentals run in the same ballpark. Just about the only person who can plan to attend a week in advance is the driver of a motorhome or camper van or the owner of a lightplane who either spends one day or can survive living in a tent under his wing for the days he wishes to attend (Figs. 5-68 and 5-69). The single-day visitor should be current on night flight since the field doesn't open until after 7:00 p.m., and long lines of departing aircraft usually assure a night takeoff and subsequent night flight in frequently challenging weather to your destination. Some aircraft were reportedly lost while flying from Oshkosh at night.

TIPS

What did we learn from our first visit to Oshkosh? In order of their importance we found out that:

(1) Get yourself in shape for a lot of walking.

(2) Bring comfortable shoes.

(3) Pack a raincoat and a sun umbrella because that crazy, mixed-up Wisconsin summer weather really doesn't know what it'll do next—and the local weather prognosticators aren't much help. Forecast thunderstorms were missing more often than not, and severe clear produced buckets of rain.

(4) Bring more cash rather than credit cards. While "plastic money" was acceptable in many booths for larger purchases and in many local stores, many others did not honor credit cards. The

Fig. 5-65. Miss EAA 1980, Sue Chambers of Minneapolis.

Fig. 5-66. The flight line and pit area is limited to registered EAA members and qualified aviation visitors. No children under 14 without a registered adult.

Fig. 5-67. The communications center has roof-top facilities for interviews with interesting aviation personalities.

Fig. 5-68. Camping area for transient visitors; everything from Cherokees to Learjets.

Fig. 5-69. Hardy visitors living in the Classic camp-out area hang their clothes out to dry under the wing of their Cessna 170B after a particularly wet night.

biggest, and perhaps best pizza house in Oshkosh, Baxter's Beef and Pizza Co., didn't take a *single* credit card—but the food was good.

(5) If you plan to camp out beneath your aircraft and get closer to the action, bring a waterproof tent, cots for all concerned to get off the not-so-waterproof floor, strong tiedowns for the tent, one-each flashlight to make your way "down the hall" which can well be a quarter of a mile to the nearest port-a-potty and the shower.

(6) Bring cameras and *plenty* of film, though local vendors have supplies available (Fig. 5-70).

(7) Carry both suntan lotion and mosquito repellent.

(8) Bring camp stools, aluminum lawn furniture, or whatever, so that you can get off your feet to watch the daily airshow. Other items in evidence were binoculars and head coverings of all types and descriptions.

The EAA meeting at Oshkosh is clean and it is "dry!" Visitors are urged to pick up everything that they drop, from cigarette butts to gum wrappers. The sprawling grounds at the Oshkosh airport are immaculate, even after a week of extremely heavy traffic. It's so contagious, the clean-up crews expected after every large public gathering are really not needed in volume at Oshkosh. In addition, there's a sign by the front door that admonishes *No alcohol and no dogs* (Fig. 5-71). While you may see an occasional beer in the camping areas after the airshow, we didn't see a single person who was obviously under the influence. And in this day and age, that isn't shabby at all.

Oshkosh is a continuing happening. A standard joke among EAAers is that on any homebuilder's divorce settlement, the pilot will try for the custody of the motel reservations for Oshkosh the following year. The Motel 6 where we stayed had a sign on the counter, "No more reservations accepted for 1981!" by the second day of the show. Local residents open their houses to roomers. Many visitors land at outlying airports where they can get a rental car and drive the remaining 50 miles to Oshkosh. Many commute up to 100 miles in rental cars. Many plan their vacations for Oshkosh and bring a camper or RV to park in designated areas—clean, green and near all the required amenities, just outside the airport fence. For pilots living in the midwest, this is a good way to go. The dormitories at the University of Wisconsin at Oshkosh are a very popular housing solution with good food,

Fig. 5-70. Everyone has a camera at Oshkosh—or should have.

Fig. 5-71. Sign at the main gate to the EAA show spells out "No dogs. No alcohol." For the most part, this rule was adhered to and the grounds were immaculately clean all the time with EAA self-policing the area.

reasonable rates, city bus transportation, laundry facilities and, a full entertainment program on the grounds.

OSHKOSH FEVER

Oshkosh fever is contagious. EAA member Fran Kadonsky (Fig. 5-72) of Libertyville, Illinois, flies the EAA helicopter (Fig. 5-73) daily during the week-long show. He plans his vacation to take this no-pay job every year; his regular job is flying Lockheed 1011s for TWA.

All the EAA help is strictly volunteer. According to the program, professional airshow talent is also on a volunteer basis; just to appear at Oshkosh is the compensation.

There are some fabulous quotes to be heard. In the FAA control tower, for example, an unnamed controller said, "None of this is legal. There are a helluva lot of waivers here today." *LIFE* Magazine assignment photographer Dan McCoy of New Jersey commented, "This is the smoothest run show I've ever seen." One homebuilder said, "Oshkosh is a shot in the arm for me. I'll come back from here and work like fury on my homebuilt 'til about Christmas. Then I'll slow up and taper off in the Spring. I've gotta come back to Oshkosh to get another shot in the arm."

NOAA provided weather briefers in a small, frequently crowded temporary office building in front of the tower. Dr. Richard E. Hallgren, Director of NOAA's National Weather Service, said, "Our primary concern is to provide a watch for severe weather to help protect the many exhibitors, competitors and spectators in these events along with their valuable aircraft."

The severe storm that passed through the area on Thursday evening near the end of the show was more than enough to get your attention. The TV at the motel told of severe weather passing eastward at 35 knots, with high winds and tornadoes in the vicinity. After we paddled out to our 170B on Friday morning and found that it was still securely tied down and right side up, we loaded our gear and headed for the weather center.

The color TV in the temporary NOAA office showed selected areas and outlined the echoes that were "painted" around significant weather. Yes, it makes quite a painting. However, westbound it was good as the weather chased its tail to the east. The thunderstorms we dodged near Cheyenne, Wyoming, the next day were nowhere to be seen on the Oshkosh radar.

At the pilots' briefing booth in front of the tower (Fig. 5-74), an EAA volunteer told us to use "wing-walkers" taxiing from our parking spaces and to be careful of the puddles. Takeoffs were on Runway 18 with flight restricted to 500 feet to the perimeter road. There, a left turn was called for by a departure turn to on course. The briefer gave us a small piece of pasteboard with a big "D" scribbled on it to prove to ground helpers that we'd had that day's briefing.

We ran a very careful pre-flight inspection because a week of "tire kickers" and interested spectators could leave unexpected problems. Everything seemed shipshape, so we untied the bird, climbed aboard and touched our air horns in lieu of hollering "Clear." (Our 170B has an FAA-approved set of Masaratti air horns forward of the firewall that is just great for calling the gas boy or assuring that children, dogs and others are not near the prop.) The Lycoming fired on the first rotation, evidently eager to get back into the air. A shower of water erupted from the starter housing as the 180 horses began to purr.

We taxied out slowly over the very wet, spongy grass, picking our way around the deeper puddles (Fig. 5-75). An EAA volunteer with a bright day-glo vest appeared and walked our wing as far as the perimeter of the classic parking area. Then the flagman asked

Fig. 5-72. Paul and Audrey Poberezny prepare for a survey flight with pilot Fran Kadonsky. Kadonsky is also a trustee of the EAA Air Museum Foundation.

Fig. 5-73. EAA helicopter used for policing and authorized aerial photography is flown annually by Fran Kadonsky of Libertyville, Illinois. He plans his vacations for this week off from flying a Lockheed 1011 for TWA.

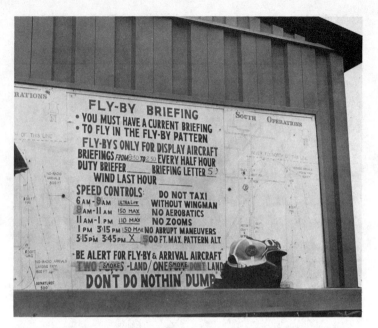

Fig. 5-74. Pilot briefing booth for fly-bys was manned daily by EAA volunteers. Here's where you get your final departure briefing. Note the bottom line, and it isn't bad at all. "Don't do nothin' dumb."

Fig. 5-75. Spongy grass made for slow taxiing as pilots queue up to depart. VariEze taxies in after a fly-by as an Ercoupe heads for the takeoff end of Runway 18 as seen from the authors' Cessna.

Fig. 5-76. All in all, drainage was excellent at Oshkosh. After a particularly heavy downpour, puddles like this collected early in the day in some areas of the flight line.

that one of us walk the wing the remainder of the way toward the flight line. Julia was the one who got her shoes wet.

We taxied around even deeper puddles with caution (Fig. 5-76). The pilot of a BD-4 that we met later that evening in Worthington, Minnesota, admitted that his homebuilt nosed up in the mud just enough to ding the prop tips, but he inspected them and allowed that they were okay to fly. Guess he was correct because he'd logged about 400 miles without a problem.

Flagmen continued to direct us. We had listened to ATIS and ground control and were given the standard, "Don't call us, we'll call you" routine. Our daisy chain of departing aircraft led to the midfield run-up area of Runway 18. A quick mag check, prop exercise, recheck for control freedom, and we were ready for what was literally a wave off.

Take off, cross the freeway, turn left and remain below 500 feet. Depart the area and climb on course. It was all very simple.

Perhaps the best recommendation we could give is the reservation we're sending to the University of Wisconsin for a room in their dorms for 1981. With a rate of $14 per day (double), 50¢ bus rides, and meals reportedly excellent and plentiful, you can't beat it.

See you at Oshkosh again!

EST AVIATION EVENT
RT AVIATION EXHIBITION
E CLASSIC ⚠ WARBIRDS

6

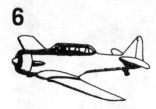

Oshkosh Scrapbook

No book can adequately describe the happening at Oshkosh each August when the EAA Fly-In/Convention takes place. Too many things are happening simultaneously throughout the week-long event. The statistics are impressive—425,000 people; more than 10,000 airplanes, 1,543 registered show planes, 858 overseas visitors from 46 countries—but the numbers do not capture the atmosphere, the essence of the EAA at Oshkosh.

The following pages offer random impressions captured on film. But if you want to capture the smell of adventure for yourself, you will have to go there and stick you head into the cockpit of an ancient biplane and inhale that lovely mixture of gasoline and aircraft dope and leather and sweat; you will have to go there to hear the heart-quickening sound of a Merlin engine, or feel the "vibes" the throaty power from a Double Wasp can induce in your very bones. You will just have to go there to appreciate the remarkable little flying machines created in garages and basements across America by people like yourself; and to experience first-hand the all-pervading euphoria, the easy rapport with all these strangers who aren't strangers at all—just thousands of the world's nicest people who speak your language and share your dreams. This is an unique gathering, unlike any other anywhere, and it constitutes *the greatest air show on earth.*

Fig. 6-1. After ceremonies were completed with the Laird Super Solution, both Matty Laird and Jimmy Doolittle went "around the patch" in the EAA's replica of the "Spirit of St. Louis" and the Stinson that accompanied the replica on a nationwide tour celebrating the 50th anniversary of Lindbergh's flight.

Fig. 6-2. Ryan and Stinson at Oshkosh. Laird and Doolittle airborne together again. Duane Cole's venerable clipped-wing Taylorcraft waits on the ramp for show time.

Fig. 6-3. Replica of the famed "Spirit of St. Louis" is kept by the EAA at Oshkosh. It was flown several times during the annual fly-in. This is one of three replicas built for the motion picture on Lindbergh's New York to Paris flight. This particular aircraft was built in Pacoima, California, by the late W.H. "Hank" Coffin and was purchased from the Tallman Air Museum and donated to the EAA.

Fig. 6-4. Replica of the Gee Bee Model Z Sportster which swept the 1931 National Air Races and took the Thompson Trophy with an average speed of 236 mph.

Fig. 6-5. A trio of Trimotors: Stinson Model A, Ford 5-AT and Junkers Ju 52. Most EAAers were not yet born when these planes were built.

Fig. 6-6. Leo Loudenslager takes off in his Lazer. Loudenslager, a 36-year old airline pilot, would return to Oshkosh the last two weeks of August to win the gold medal in the World Aerobatics Championship.

Fig. 6-7. Duane Cole's clipped-wing T-Craft is framed by the wings of a Stearman show plane. The old master still performs his famed dead-stick acro routine.

Fig. 6-8. A Lockheed 12A Electra, built in 1937, is similar to the airplane in which Amelia Earhart disappeared over the Pacific.

Fig. 6-9. Replica of Doolittle's famous Laird Super Solution is complete except for wheel pants; joins EAA permanent aircraft display.

Fig. 6-10. A like-new Aeronca K, part of the EAA permanent display.

160

Fig. 6-11. Funk B85C flown by William and Richard King of Rhinebeck, New York.

Fig. 6-12. The two-place Cessna 140, produced from 1946 to 1951, was powered with both the 85 and 90-hp Continental, the former had fabric-covered wings. Normal cruise is 105 mph.

Fig. 6-13. Ryan SC of 1939 is two-place, cruises at 135 mph with a 145-hp Warner radial engine.

162

Fig. 6-14. Don Stretch, VP at Airtex, the major producer of pre-fitted lightplane interiors, is also president of the Ercoupe Club.

163

Fig. 6-15. Luscombe Silvaire; the first ones, with 50-75 hp, were built 1937-1940. Post-war versions had 65, 85 and 90-hp as the 8A, 8E and 8F models. TEMCO took over production in 1950, and a Colorado company produced some 90-hp versions between 1955 and 1960. Therefore, a Silvaire may be an antique, classic or modern airplane.

Fig. 6-16. Classic Cessna 195 at Oshkosh with wash hung out to dry on its radio antennas. Not an unusual sight.

Fig. 6-17. The four-place Cessna Airmasters were built 1934-1940 inclusive with Warner radials of 145 and 165-hp; were the forerunners of the post-war 190/195s.

Fig. 6-18. It was possible to view most of the air show activities from the parking area for Classic aircraft. Lines of parked aircraft did not obscure the smoky 450-hp Stearmans making low passes with a stuntman (frequently a woman) strapped atop the top wing.

Fig. 6-19. The 125-hp Ryan was built as a USAAF trainer (PT-20), and also sold in the civilian market as the STA sport plane.

Fig. 6-20. Exact replica (except for tailwheel) of the Travel Air Model S "Mystery Ship" which won the 1929 Thompson Race and influenced future fighter aircraft design.

Fig. 6-21. See? There really is a completed BD-5.

Fig. 6-22. The Acapella by Option Air Reno claims 196 mph with a 100-hp Continental 0-200; 285 mph with the IO-360 Lycoming of 200-hp. Acapella is a successful attempt to make a flyable aircraft from orphaned BD-5 parts.

Fig. 6-23. John Dyke designed the unusual four-place Dyke Delta; Dale Lincoln of Dayton, Ohio, built this one. Over two dozen Dyke Deltas are presently flying.

Fig. 6-24. A Christen Eagle II arrives carrying an auxiliary smoke pod.

Fig. 6-25. Another nice Canadian homebuilt, the J-3 Eagle built in 1980.

Fig. 6-26. The Eagle's engine is a Porsche 35.

Fig. 6-27. Don Taylor of Hemet, California flew his T-18 homebuilt around the world.

Fig. 6-28. This EAA Acrosport, powered with an 0-320 engine, was built by Fred Dangler of Palo Alto, California, and the information card on its propeller contains the remark, "I told my wife it cost only $3,000."

Fig. 6-29. The modern Great Lakes, back in production as this is written, is essentially the same airframe as the original, which was produced 1929 through 1933, although today's version employs a modern engine and materials.

Fig. 6-30. A few homebuilt owners erect barriers to ward off sticky fingerprints and other manifestations of interest.

Fig. 6-31. The ever-popular Wittman Tailwind.

Fig. 6-32. The EOS/SFA-1 cross-country sport plane is single-place and powered with a 1,834-cc VW engine. Cruising speed is given as 180 mph at 75 percent power. The literature warns that "it is not intended to be the simplest aircraft to construct."

Fig. 6-33. A CAP 21, French import designed for unlimited aerobatics.

Fig. 6-34. A BD-8 with 180-hp 0-360 Lycoming engine; owned by Mike Huffman of Owasso, Oklahoma.

Fig. 6-35. The helicopter pad is at the south end of the field; homebuilt Scorpion in flight.

Fig. 6-36. The EOS/SFA-1 (Fig. 6-32) engine is the Revmaster conversion of the 1,834-cc Volkswagen.

Fig. 6-37. A very nice Thorp T-18 built by Ron Zimmerman in 1967 and fitted with a 135-hp Lycoming 0-290D-2 engine.

Fig. 6-38. Folding-wing Bushby Mustang II is built from component kits; either one or two-place, with a wide range of engines possible.

Fig. 6-39. Seaplane pilots have their own cook-out going in their area. Homebuilt Ospery II amphibian in foreground.

Fig. 6-40. Rand-Robinson KR-1 cruises at 180 mph with a 1700-cc VW engine; weighs 375 lbs empty. Wing span is 17 ft.

Fig. 6-41. Thorp T-18s. This outstanding two-place design has been around since the mid-sixties and still popular because of the simplicity of its all-metal construction and excellent performance. It has 180-hp and cruises at 175 mph. Note that N23GA has Bonanza-like V-tail.

Fig. 6-42. Two-way traffic. Half-scale W.A.R. Corsairs and a VariEze.

Fig. 6-43. A pair of apparently identical EAA Acrosports from Cadillac, Michigan.

Fig. 6-44. The Jeffair Barracuda is an all-wood high-performance two-placer designed for ease of building and serious cross-country flying. It will accept engines of 180 to 300-hp, and has an estimated building time of 2,000 hours.

Fig. 6-45. The two-place Sidewinder, designed by Jerry Smyth, has 125-hp.

Fig. 6-46. This Davis DA-2A, powered with a 100-hp Continental, was flown by Ed van Belkam of Neenah, Wisconsin.

Fig. 6-47. An EAA Acrosport biplane owned by Dorothy Aiksnoras.

Fig. 6-48. The VW-powered Dragonfly, apparently inspired by the Quickie, is two-place, claims a cruise of 155 mph. It is not a Rutan design.

Fig. 6-49. The MiniBat is launched by tow, but has a three-hp chainsaw engine that takes over to sustain flight once airborne. Built by Larry Haig of Muskegon, Michigan. Note tiny prop at fuselage/rudder juncture.

Fig. 6-50. The American Eage was built by Bruce Shannon of Bethlehem, Pennsylvania. Power is a McCullough 101 of 12-hp.

Fig. 6-51. Dick Rutan arrives in a Long-EZ, flying non-stop from San Francisco. A WW-II TBM Navy torpedo bomber in background.

Fig. 6-52. This Rutan Long-EZ flew to Oshkosh non-stop from Florida.

Fig. 6-53. This strictly unofficial sign marked a long line of Rutan VariEzes at Oshkosh.

Fig. 6-54. The four-place Rutan Defiant probably should be described as a current state-of-the-art machine compared to the commercially produced light twins which many feel are 25 years behind the times.

Fig. 6-55. The twin engine "push-pull" Rutan Defiant (foreground), a Rutan VariViggen, and a gaggle of VariEzes.

Fig. 6-56. Christen Eagle I takes off to participate in aerobatic show. The two-place Eagle II is offered in a series of kits that require approximately 1,400 hours building time with no welding.

Fig. 6-57. Mike Sorrell's two-place Hyperbipe is a high performance craft with 180-hp and stressed for aerobatics. Hyperbipe is available only in kit form.

Fig. 6-58. Moon Maid is an original design powered with a VW engine and completed in 1964 by Richard Doyle of Mt. Prospect, Illinois.

Fig. 6-59. Restored WWII advanced trainers, Air Force T-6G (foreground) and Navy SNJ. The "Texan" was also built in Canada as the Harvard IV.

Fig. 6-60. Lineup of North American P-51D and K Mustangs, with Bell P-63 sneaking in (third from camera). B-17 and B-25 in background. First Mustang in line is painted in colors of famous 4th Fighter Group of WWII.

Fig. 6-61. A Confederate Air Force B-17 flies the Texas flag in the warbird area.

Fig. 6-62. Everyone turns out to watch the EAA's own B-17 arrive. A recent addition to the EAA museum, this Fort is appropriately named "Aluminum Overcast."

195

Fig. 6-63. This beautifully restored Boeing-Stearman was a PT-17 in Army Air Force dress, an N2S-3 as a U.S. Navy trainer during WWII.

Fig. 6-64. Bucker Jungmann was a Luftwaffe training plane prior to and during WWII, which makes it an authentic warbird or antique.

Fig. 6-65. The EAA's Lockheed T-33 jet trainer on permanent display in the Camp Scholler area. First flown as the TF-80 during the Korean War, the "T-Bird" still serves on with many USAF units. A few are even owned and operated by serious (and affluent) Warbirders.

Fig. 6-66. W.A.R. Corsairs and a classic Stinson Station Wagon wait for B-17 to clear runway.

Fig. 6-67. A "soft-nose" B-25J with guns in place. Restoration costs on such an aircraft can easily exceed $100,000.

Fig. 6-68. Noted av-writer Martin Caidin, who created *The Six Million Dollar Man*, was at Oshkosh with his lovingly restored Junkers Ju-52. Caidin tells the fascinating story of this airplane and its restoration in *The Saga of Iron Annie* (Doubleday, 1979).

Fig. 6-69. D-Day, 1944? No, Oshkosh 1980. Six immaculate Mustangs taxi in train.

Fig. 6-70. The Boeing B-17G Flying Fortress donated to the EAA Museum by Dr. Bill Harrison and Dr. Al Shirkey, Tulsa, OK; Max Hoffman, Ft. Collins, CO; Scott Smith, Orlando, FL; George Enhorning, Wolcott, CT; and Tom Camp, San Francisco, CA. Prosit, gentlemen!

Fig. 6-71. Many refurbished warbirds are painted to represent a specific aircraft that saw combat in WWII. This Mustang has been restored as *Double Trouble* of the 8th Air Force's 353rd Fighter Group.

Fig. 6-72. The U.S. Navy pays its respects. The Navy also sent a Marine Harrier, the VTOL fighter, which won the unofficial award as the noisiest aircraft at Oshkosh.

Fig. 6-73. Look again—it's not a Stearman! This is the Navy's N3N WWII primary trainer, built by the Naval Aircraft Factory.

Fig. 6-74. A Douglas C-47 (Skytrain or Gooney Bird, or Dakota to the British) painted with invasion stripes for the Normandy invasion of Europe, 1944. B-25 Mitchell in background.

Fig. 6-75. Rare Curtis P-40Es; craft at left is painted in the colors of the famed American Volunteer Group, better known as the "Flying Tigers," specifically, the 2nd squadron, "Panda Bears."

Fig. 6-76. Warbirds in formation. A full house of AT-6s make a fly-by during one of the EAA airshows.

Fig. 6-77. A tight formation of T-6s suggests that some of their pilots were military trained.

Fig. 6-78. A rare and inspiring sight—three Boeing B-17s in formation.

Fig. 6-79. The Twin Lazair, by Dale Cramer of Port Colborne, Ontario Canada, is powered by a pair of six-hp Pioneer P-60 Peach engines.

Fig. 6-80. Study in contrasts; a Learjet and the ultralight Eagle which is sold ready to fly ($3,395), and is assembled/disassembled for car-top transportation in 30 minutes without tools.

Fig. 6-81. The Fisher Flyer employs beefed-up Easy Riser wings and is powered by a 30-hp Xenoh engine. Construction time was two months, by Mike Fisher of South Webster, Ohio.

Fig. 6-82. Engine compartment of the 240-lb Fisher Flyer. Total cost was under $2,000.

Fig. 6-83. The popular Easy Riser resulted when Taras Kiceniuk's Icarus II hang glider was given a tiny engine. Lightweight wheels aid in ground handling.

Fig. 6-84. Oshkosh is not limited to homebuilt aircraft. Most general aviation manufacturers display here annually. The Beechcraft display is shown here.

Fig. 6-85. A United L-1011 is here for inspection by interested EAAers.

Fig. 6-86. We follow a couple of floatplanes in a "fly-by."

Fig. 6-87. A 1929 Curtiss Robin is part of the EAA Museum's display near the main entrance.

Fig. 6-88. Traffic jam. A pair of Monnett Formula V (VW-powered) sport/racers maneuver between Rutan's Defiant, VariViggen and Long-EZ, while a Piper Cub awaits its turn.

Fig. 6-89. J. J. Frey of the Edo Float Company is here to commune with the seaplane pilots.

Fig. 6-90. The homebuilt aircraft repair area at Oshkosh; small problems quickly solved.

Fig. 6-91. Midwest humorist put up this sign beside a large puddle following heavy rains.

Fig. 6-92. EAA helicopter was used solely to patrol the airport, advise of parking spaces for aircraft and cars, coordinate with security and provide an occasional press flight.

Fig. 6-93. A hot air balloon remains on a tether; too much air traffic to allow him to float free.

Fig. 6-94. The Super Aero 45, produced by the Czechoslovokian Aircraft Works, has two Walter Minor 4-111 engines of 105-hp each. Cruising speed is 125 kits. It is owned by Jon Svendsen of Waterloo, Iowa.

Fig. 6-95. The seaplane base at Oshkosh is just east of the airport on Lake Winnebago.

Fig. 6-96. Interested in a portable airplane hangar? The Port-A-Port Company shows off its Executive I model with overhead doors.

Fig. 6-97. A pair of Stearmans perform with wing riders. Classic area is deserted as everyone moves closer to the action.

Fig. 6-98. The aerobatic show starts at four p.m. each afternoon.

Fig. 6-99. George Varga, a WW-II pilot, explaining his Varga Kachina to an interested EAAer. Ironically, the Kachina, now a production aircraft, began life itself as a homebuilt.

Fig. 6-100. The Wing Derringer, two-place twin, announced several years ago, is still planned for commercial production.

Index